LIVE to be a 100

Essential Medical Sense for this Technological Age

Sickness-free through Awareness.
All the medical knowledge a layman would need to live well in this technological age

Dr PK's Holistic Medico Advisory. The book.
A compendium of useful medical life-style info that could improve your life and health considerably.

From the "Posts and Sharings" from my Facebook Page.

By Pradeep Maheshwari
Email: gururdeva@yahoo.com
Contact for consulting:
Thanks and Regards
PK(Pradeep Maheshwari)- S164-Greater Kailash Part 1. New Delhi 110048
intro to latest book/activities: http://carecompassionmedicine.weebly.com
phone: **91-11-41730043,**
skype:pradeepmahesh. Facebook: Pradeep PK Maheshwari

Foreword by the author

Over the years, I have found that I am repeating certain pointers over and over again. Technology has brought in changes and we need to change some of our working ideas but that is not always happening and this is causing a lot of disequilibrium in health issues. For example, doctors still advise in rural India to boil the feed bottle for babies but the bottles have changed from glass or stainless-steel ones to plastic. This makes boiling dangerous.

What becomes obvious is that people have been adopting products and practices by following "tradition" and believing the advertising with a lot of trust in the goodwill of the marketing or/and manufacturing companies, just as they would have or did the local Mom-Pop shops and ventures.

Similar looking and named/tasting products that are slow-death-bombs now flood the markets. Good advertising has brain-washed people into accepting them as better alternatives. Example: Margarine for butter; Carbonated drinks for soda; Hydrogenated oil for butter-oil; soap is replaced by detergent and so on.

Additionally the body wants known and established habits and the straight and narrow path of undisturbed equilibrium. The mind needs the opposite to grow and expand. Stresses and strains of life and the information over-load are so disorienting.

The reality has changed and most of us are not fully in tune with it. Quite obviously we need to be appraised of it. It is clear that people are not looking for exhaustive treatises. So I have put all my basic knowledge and experience on this subject into this compilation that addresses this need "to know the most pertinent, easily adoptable minimum information" that if understood and put into practice will definitely bring change in the well being and general health status of people.

This book is purposely a short read. I understand that every subject covered may not be of interest to everybody. So once I have got you thinking, please take time out to read more on the subjects. Every word has been selected to convey precisely what I want to say without going into long dissertations. I hope it helps.

1) **Let us begin with how our food affects our health.**

The body takes in more than 40 elements from outside of it, mainly through food, to sustain itself in good vibrant health. It then forms thousands of compounds as it needs to repair and maintain itself. The body has all the knowledge – all it needs is that it is supplied all the ingredients properly. This is why selective eating as one can see with individuals can create specific deficiencies which then easily get transmuted to disease. In many families certain eating habits are passed down generation after generation; these are often called genetically passed on but I have noticed by changing food habits immediate changes are visible. So our duty is to eat well and balanced meals, with a lot of variety in our life. Most important: Feed your body for your health and not for "TASTE".

99% of people eat for satisfying their palate. I can only call this a serious lack of applied intelligence. They eat certain foods to exclusivity and do not realize that they are piling up a debt that they will have to pay later with interest in the form of pain and financial losses with hospitalization and eventually early death.

FAQs The Symptoms of Nutrient Deficiencies
(taken from: http://revivelifelab.com/kids/vitality-balance-kids-%E2%84%A2/faqs-the-symptoms-of-nutrient-deficiencies/)

Vitamins & Minerals Chart

Fat Soluble Vitamins (A, D, E, K) can be stored in the body and need not be consumed daily. While it is difficult to "overdose" on them from ordinary sources, consuming mega doses of fat soluble vitamins, especially A and D, can lead to a dangerous build up in the body.

Abbreviations: IU=International Units; mg=milligrams; mcg=micrograms.

Vitamin/ Mineral	Source	Indication	Efficacy	Claims
Vitamin A Retinol	Liver, fortified	Eyes (Night	**Deficiency:**Night blindness; reduced	Assists body in ridding

Men: 3 000 IU Women: 2 700 IU	Milk (Retinol form – see below for Carotene sources.)	Vision) Skin Hair Bones Teeth Immune System Liver Reproductive Organs Pregnancy & Lactation	hair growth in children; loss of apetite; dry, rough skin; lowered resistance to infection; dry eyes. **Overdose:**Headaches; blurred vision; fatigue; diarrhea; irregular periods; joint and bone pain; dry, cracked skin; rashes; loss of hair; vomiting, liver damage	environmental pollutants
Beta Carotene (Pro-Vitamin A) (See Vitamin A)	Alfalfa sprouts, Avocado, Bannana, Bee pollen, Brocolli, Cayenne pepper, Carrots Yellow orange fruit, Garlic, Squash, Broccoli, Green & Yellow Vegetables	Antioxidant. Converted to Vitamin A in the body. (See Vitamin A)		The antioxidant properties of this nutrientmay be a factor in reducing the risk of certain forms of cancer.
Vitamin D Men: 100 IU Women: 100 IU	Egg Yolk, Milk, Exposure to sun enables body to make its own	Teeth & Bones Immunity Enhances calcium & phosphorus absorption.	**Deficiency:**Rickets in children; bone softening in adults; osteoporosis. **Overdose:**Calcium deposits in organs; fragile bones; renal	

	Vitamin D., Cod liver Oil, Salmon, seeds, lemongrass, dandelion root, alfalfa sprouts, avocado, garlic, greens leafy	Regulates mineral absorption Stabilizes nervous system & heart Normal blood clotting	and cardiovascular damage.	
Vitamin E Men: 9-10 mg Women: 6-7 mg	Corn or Cottonseed Oil, Butter, Brown Rice, Soybean Oil, Vegetable oils such as Corn, Cottonseed or Soybean, Nuts Wheat Germ.	Antioxidant. Helps form red blood cells, muscles and other tissues. Preserves fatty acids. Reproduction Lacation RBC protection Wounds Prevention blood clots	**Deficiency:**Rare, seen primarily in premature or low birth weight babies or children who do not absorb fat properly. Causes nerve abnormalities. **Overdose:**Unknown.	The antioxidant properties of this nutrient may be a factor in reducing the risk of certain forms of cancer
Vitamin K None established. Estimated at 0.03 mcg/kg	Green Vegetables, Liver, also made by intestinal bacteria.	Needed for normal blood clotting.	**Deficiency:** Defective blood coagulation. **Overdose:**Jaundice in infants.	

Water Soluble Vitamins are not stored in the body and should therefore be consumed daily.

Thiamine **Vitamin B1** Men: 0.8 – 1.3 mg	Sunflower Seeds, Pork, whole and enriched	Carbohydrate metabolism Muscle	**Deficiency:** Anxiety; hysteria; depression; muscle cramps; loss of	

Women: 0.8 mg	Grains, dried Beans., kelp, dates, garlic, parsley, wild rice, watercress, wheatgrass	coordination. Proper nerve function. **VIP consistent growth in children** Helps with Stress Stabilizes appetite by improving digestion and assimilation of nutrients Fertility & Lactation Provides Energy Mental attitude , focus & concentration	appetite; in extreme cases beriberi (mostly in alcoholics). **Overdose:** Unknown, although excess of one B vitamin may cause deficiency of others.
Riboflavin Vitamin B2 Men: 1.3 – 1.6 mg Women: 1.1 mg	Liver, Milk, Spinach, enriched Noodles, Mushrooms., alfalfa sprouts, apple , apricot, avocado, dates, figs, garlic, kelp, parsley, wild rice rosehips, seeds	Needed for metabolism of all foods and the release of energy to cells. Essential to the functioning of Vitamin B6 and Niacin. RBCs & antibodies Vision Skin, nails ,	**Deficiency:**Cracks and sores around the mouth and nose; visual problems. **Overdose:** See Vitamin B1

		hair Stress	
Niacin **Vitamin B3** Men: 16-23 mg Women: 14-16 mg Niacin is converted to niacinamide in the body.	Mushrooms, Bran, Tuna, Chicken, Beef, Peanuts, enriched Grains., rice brown, wild , alfalfa, almonds, apricots, chamomile, figs, garlic, nuts	Needed in many enzymes that convert food to energy. Helps maintain a healthy digestive tract and nervous system. In very large doses, lower cholesterol (large doses should only be taken under the advice of a physician).	**Deficiency:** In extreme cases, pellagra, a disease characterized by dermatitis, diarrhea and mouth sores. **Overdose:** Hot flashes; ulcers; liver disorders; high blood sugar and uric acid; cardiac arrythmias
Pantothenic Acid **Vitamin B5** Men: 2.5 mg Women: 2.5 mg	Abundant in animal tissues, whole grain cereals and legumes., alfalfa, almonds, avocado, broccoli, honey faw, oats, oranges, peas, seeds, soybeans, walnuts	Converts food to molecular forms. Needed to manufacture adrenal hormones and chemicals that regulate nerve function. Wounds Adrenals Produced in the body by the beneficial bacteria in the intestines	**Deficiency:** Unclear in humans. **Overdose:** See Vitamin B
Vitamin B6	Animal	Protein	**Deficiency:**

Pyridoxine Men: 1.8 mg Women: 1.5 mg	protein foods, Spinach, Broccoli, Bananas, alfalfa, bell pepper, beets, cantaloupe, greens, lemon, nuts,peas, sprouts, veggies green	metabolism and absorption Carbohydrate metabolism. Helps form red blood cells. Promotes nerve and brain function. Skin , Teeth, muscles , nerves Antibodies, RBCs Balance of Sodium & Phosphorus, Balance of Sodium & Potassium	Anemia, irritability, patches of itchy, scaling skin; convulsions. **Overdose:** Nerve damage.
Vitamin B12 Cyanocobalamin Men: 2 mcg Women: 2 mcg	Found almost exclusively in animal products, alfalfa, beans, dulse, garlic, Korean, Siberian ginseng, klep, nuts, seeds,	Builds genetic material. Helps form red blood cells. Growth Energy RBC s Concentration, memory , balance	**Deficiency:** Pernicious anemia; nerve damage. (Note: Deficiency rare except in strict vegetarians, the elderly or people with malabsorption disorders.) **Overdose:** See Vitamin B1.
Biotin 60 mcg	Cheese, Egg, Yolk, Cauliflower, Peanut Butter,	Needed for metabolism of glucose and formation of certain fatty	**Deficiency:** Seborrhic dermatitis in infants. Rare in adults, but can be induced by consuming large

	alfalfa sprouts, banana , beans, fruits, grains, nuts ,brown rice, seeds, soybeans	acids. Essential for proper body chemistry. Formation RNA & DNA Food into energy Prevent exhaustion Muscle pain Helps prevent baldness	amounts of egg whites – anorexia, nausea, vomiting, dry scaly skin. **Overdose:** See Vitamin B1	
Folic Acid(Folacin) Men: 180-220 mg Women: 160-190 mg	Green, leafy vegetables, Orange Juice, organ Meats, Sprouts.	Essential for the manufacture of genetic material as well as protein metabolism and red blood cell formation Brain Function RBCs Circulation	**Deficiency:**Impaired cell division; anemia; diarrhea; gastrointestinal upsets. **Overdose:**Convulsions in epileptics. May mask pernicious anemia (see Vitamin B12 deficiency).	Adequate amounts of this nutrient in the firststage of pregnancymay reduce the risks of neural tube birth defects.
Vitamin C Ascorbic Acid Men: 40 mg Women: 30 mg	Citrus Fruits, Strawberries, Broccoli, Green Peppers	Antioxidant. Helps bind cells together and strengthens blood vessel walls. Helps maintain healthy gums. Aids in the absorption of iron.	**Deficiency:**Muscle weakness, bleeding gums; easy bruising. In extreme cases, scurvy. **Overdose:**Loose bowls	The antioxidant properties of this nutrient may be a factor in reducing the risk of certain forms of cancer. May reduce the effects of the

		Collagen, Connective Tissue Bones, Teeth, Natural laxative Formation of adrenalin	common cold.

Minerals in organic products essential for body functions.

Calcium Men: 800 – 1000 mg Women: 700-800 mg	Milk, Yogurt, Cheese, Sardines, Broccoli, Turnip Greens.	Bones & Teeth Muscle & Nerve Function Blood Clotting Activates enzymes needed to convert food to energy	**Deficiency:**Muscle cramps, Brain function, Rickets in children; osteomalacia (soft bones) and osteoporosis in adults. **Overdose:**Constipation, Kidney Stones, calcium deposits in body tissues. Hinders absorption of iron and other minerals.
Chromium	Beets, cardamom, cloves, dulse, garlic, kelp, mushrooms, wheatgrass, onions	Glucose to Energy Metabolism of amino acids (building blocks of proteins) and fats	**Deficiency:**Glucose intolerance or insulin resistance hyperglycemia Raised serum lipids & weight changes **Overdose:**Hinders body's absorption of calcium.
Copper 2-3 mg	Liver and other organ Meats, Seafoods, Nuts and	Proteins involved in growth Nerve function Energy release	**Deficiency:** Anemia that is unresponsive to iron therapy but corrected by copper

	Sources	Functions	Deficiency / Overdose
	Seeds., pomegranates, prunes, green veggies , parslety , peas, raisins, grains, almonds , avocado	Enzymes for Iron metabolism (ceruplasmin (ferroxidase I) and ferroxidase II) Antioxidant Regulation of gene expression Component of several enzymes, including on needed to make skin, hair and other pigments. Stimulates iron absorption. Needed to make red blood cells, connective tissue and nerve fibres.	Low WBC's thus lower immunity Rare in adults. Infants may develop a type of anemia marked by abnormal development of bones, nerve tissue and lungs. **Overdose:** Liver disease; vomiting; diarrhea
Iron (Elemental) Men: 8-10 mg Women: 8-13 mg	Liver, lean Meats, Kidney beans, enriched Bread, Raisins., alfalfa sprouts, almonds, apricot, asparagus, beets, cherries, dates, figs, grains, grteens, lentils , parsley, peacans,	Essential for making hemoglobin, the red substance in blood that carries oxygen to body cells Most iron is stored in bone marrow that makes blood cells If there is not enough in the body , it goes to the bone marrow reserves. If this	**Deficiency:** Skin pallor; weakness; fatigue; headaches; shortness of breath, difficulty concentrating, brittle nails, cracked lips **Overdose:** Constipation Type II diabetes (J of A Medical Assn) Toxic buildup in liver and in rare instances the heart

	pistachio nuts, seeds, swiss chard, walnut Note: Oxalic acid in spinach hinders iron absorption.	iron stored in the bone marrow is low, RBCs don't form properly, they are smaller than usual (microcytosis) and fewer	
Magnesium Men: 230 – 250 mg Women: 200 – 210 mg	Spinach, Beef Greens, Broccoli, Tofu, Popcorn, Cashews, Wheat Bran, coconut, dates, figs, beets, avocado, honey raw,	Activates enzymes needed to release energy in body. Needed by cells for genetic material and bone growth. Low calcium Low serum potassium Retention of sodium Low circulating levels of parathyroid hormone Muscular tremors, spasms Loss of appetite, nausea, vomiting, personality changes Alkalinity Lung & Brain Function Aids digestion	**Deficiency:**Nausea, irritability, muscle weakness; twitching; cramps, cardiac arrhythmias. **Overdose:**Nausea, vomiting, low blood pressure, nervous system disorders. **Warning:**Overdose can be fatal to people with kidney disease.

Manganese 2-5 mg	Tea, whole Grains and Cereal products are the richest dietary sources. Adequate amounts are found in Fruits and Vegetables.	tendon and bone structure. Wound healing Metabolism of carbohydrates, amino acids & cholesterol Thyroid hormones	**Deficiency:** Impaired growth, reproduction, skeletal system, glucose tolerance, altered carbohydrate and lipid metabolism **Overdose:**Caution may be toxic at high doses Generally results from inhalation of manganese containing dust or fumes, not dietary ingestion.	Antioxidant
Molybdenum 0.15-0.3 mg	The concentration in food varies depending on the environment in which the food was grown. Milk, Beans, Breads and Cereals contribute the highest amounts.	Component of enzymes needed in metabolism. Helps regulate iron storage.	**Deficiency:**Unknown in humans. **Overdose:** Gout-like joint pain.	
Phosphorus Men: 1000 mg Women: 850 mg (3-6 g)	Chicken Breast, Milk, Lentils, Egg Yolks, Nuts, Cheese	With calcium builds bones and teeth. Needed for metabolism, body chemistry, nerve and muscle function	**Deficiency:**(Rare) Weakness; bone pain; Anorexia. **Overdose:**Hinders body's absorption of calcium.	
Potassium Men: 40-80 mmol Women: 40-	Peanuts, Bananas, Orange Juice, Green Beans,	Helps maintain regular fluid balance. Needed for	**Deficiency:**Nausea, anorexia, muscle weakness, irritability. (Occurs most often in	

80 mmol (3-6 g)	Mushrooms, Oranges, Broccoli, Sunflower Seeds.	nerve and muscle function.	persons with prolonged diarrhea.) **Overdose:** Rare.
Selenium 0.05-0.2 mg	Adequate amounts are found in Seafood, Kidney, Liver and other meats. Grains and other Seed contain varying amounts depending on the soil content.	Antioxidant. Interacts with Vitamin E to prevent breakdown of fats and body chemicals	**Deficiency:**Unknown in humans. **Overdose:** Finger nail changes, hair loss
Sodium		Acid neutralizer Proper fx of muscles and nerves Prevents clotting Enhances digestion	**Deficiency:** Maybe related to low blood pressure **Overdose:** May elevate blood pressure
Zinc Men: 12 mg Women: 9 mg	Oysters, Shrimp, Crab, Beef, Turkey, whole Grains, Peanuts, Beans.	Necessary element in more than 100 enzymes that are essential to digestion and metabolism	**Deficiency:** Slow healing of wounds; loss of taste; retarded growth and delayed sexual development in children. **Overdose:** Nausea, vomiting; diarrhea; abdominal pain; gastric bleeding

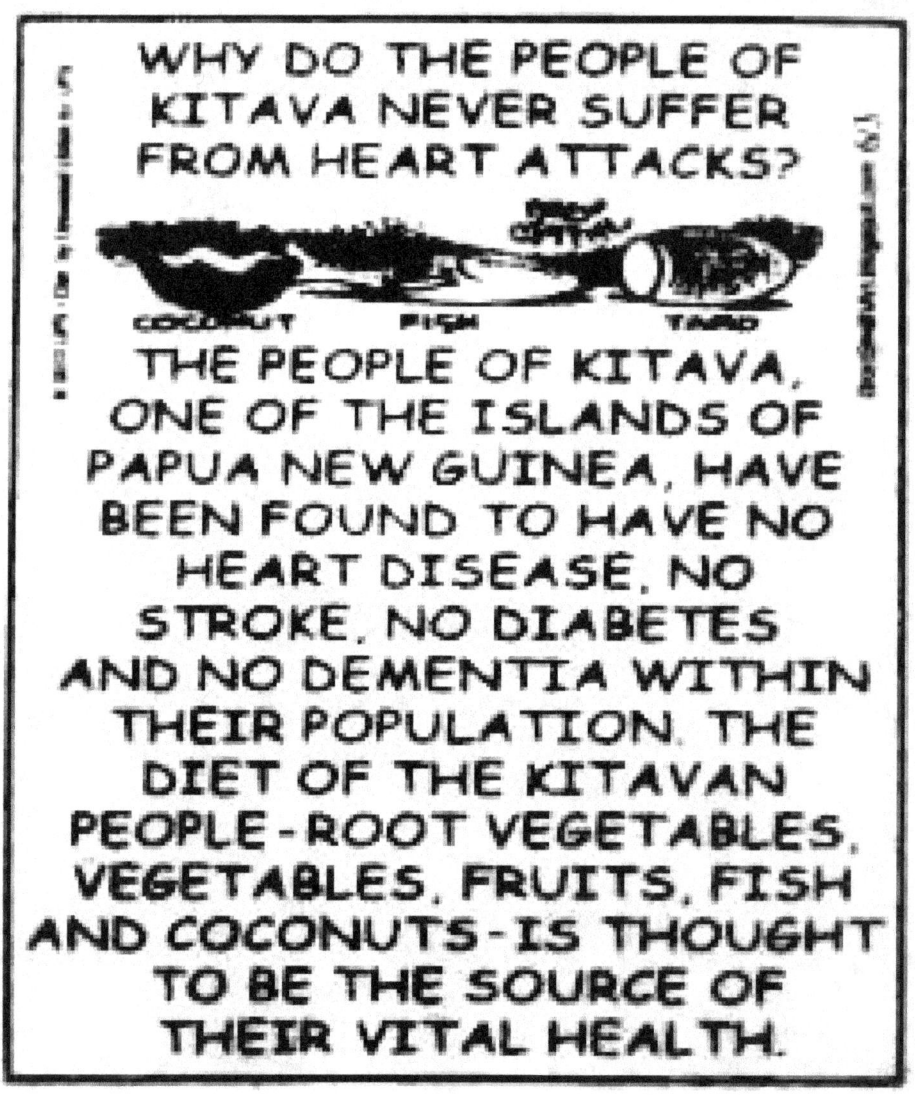

WHY DO THE PEOPLE OF KITAVA NEVER SUFFER FROM HEART ATTACKS?

COCONUT   FISH   TARO

THE PEOPLE OF KITAVA, ONE OF THE ISLANDS OF PAPUA NEW GUINEA, HAVE BEEN FOUND TO HAVE NO HEART DISEASE, NO STROKE, NO DIABETES AND NO DEMENTIA WITHIN THEIR POPULATION. THE DIET OF THE KITAVAN PEOPLE - ROOT VEGETABLES, VEGETABLES, FRUITS, FISH AND COCONUTS - IS THOUGHT TO BE THE SOURCE OF THEIR VITAL HEALTH.

.....+ they are living on an island, which means fresh sea breeze and a very clean air envelope. The water must be equally life-giving. And if they have not allowed themselves to be industrially swamped then noise pollution and over-light pollution too would not be plaguing them. Points to consider.

Ruminating on the conversation I was having on the quality of life, living older, medical assistance and developments and such stuff, I felt that we are not paying much attention to long term effects of our activities. Our approach to life is based on short term gains that clearly may not stand in good stead in the long term. In many cases we are not always aware of the consequences and we adopt practices that with looking back we realize did not help us at all; although they gave us a moment to shine with.

Let me put down some examples that come to mind:

· Protection from the weather thru heating and Air-conditioning: The body's own resistance is decreased. Sunstrokes as well as chills are striking easily and faster.

· Too much antibiotics: Difficult to treat people with natural medicines and homeopathy and such as the symptoms are not clear and the body has no vitality in it to fight back on its own.

· Too much watching things being laid out for us on gadgets: Our own researching abilities and memories have lost the edge and there is an impression of dumbing down.

· Food like factory made microwave dinners: Easy and convenient but no health benefits; rather the opposite.

· Using vehicles and machines to move about: Physical lack of use of muscles making people weak and without stamina.

From a very general view of things, all the scientific interventions made thru the brilliance of minds coming from the better educated and tech based worlds, one word stands out: "Side-effects". There are just too many and none of them praiseworthy. I think all this progress has only made people sicklier, & dumber. The argument that people are living longer is so immature - we do not have a good reason to live longer...!!

Well, in most cases, local lore has all it needs and we should adopt the old formulas from where ever we are.

India has the distinction of having every kind of medical discipline. I use formulas & preparations sold over the counter from Allopathic, Ayurvedic (the systems in the south of India are different from those of the north), Homeopathic and Unani systems +Shiatsu- together they are magic

As a naturopath I just don't see the value in many of the new drugs and therapies. As a follower of the Karmic path, I am quite comfortable with death and destiny. Sickness also pushes us to look within and develop faculties and abilities that are often amazing and needed for the evolution of this earth. So, until I fully understand the game Mother Earth is playing, I would not want to interfere too dramatically.

Conrad Cain: Whistling to sheep. Pk? I'd love to know how well this works out for you. Have you ever been able to convince one to see things any differently? I have not.

Pradeep Pk Maheshwari: It is like whistling in the forest. I do it because I like it and because it seems to annoy people - may not convince them but a shadow is left and it may have its affect long later as much as 30 years later.

Do you feel that their ways will hurt them or lead them into disaster? Then instead of getting angry at all the stupidity around you, just remove the sharp objects from their path. Let them bumble along; happy in your company. Contentment is already theirs. Why perturb them and lose our own centre of calm?

Our health is the fine result of our stresses that we impose on ourselves thru our thoughts, emotions and activities (this includes food). Do we really know; really know from the level of consciousness of the Cosmos? Yet, wanting to put the switch on is the problem. The shadows allow us to hide and what we do not see then can easily be ignored. Most of us live comfortably by the street lights that filter into our homes.

And we pay greater attention to the dark windows of the neighborhood and than ours.

Picture from: A room with a view .

2) <u>Dr PK's Holistic Medico Advisory</u> shared <u>Swami Taramani</u>'s <u>photo</u>.
<u>January 11</u>

Parks can boost mental health:

Green spaces — such as parks and gardens — in towns and cities could lead to significant and sustained improvements in mental health, according to a new study. Also, moving to a greener area not only improves people's mental health, but the effect continues long after they have moved, UK researchers found.

3) <u>Dr PK's Holistic Medico Advisory</u>
<u>January 28</u>

The Sedentary Death Syndrome
Maybe a new term to you. It has the dubious distinction of being a killer in the same class as heart disease and cancer. Unfortunately it is not a disease, medically speaking. In short it is SeDs. It is reaching epidemic proportions and many ailments like diabetes, depression, osteoporosis, certain cancers and sexual dysfunction are being attributed it. Being sedentary is a worse risk compared to smoking and hypertension. It has been researched from using the treadmill; the capacity of an individual to exercise is a far more potent indicator of good health and possibility of mortal danger than all other risk factors.
Just by becoming moderately active from a totally sedentary position, increases your chances of a healthier and better health by nearly 50%.

4) <u>Dr PK's Holistic Medico Advisory</u>
<u>January 28</u>

Feeling a mood towards the worse coming on?
Go out into the sunlight, walk a bit and think of something pleasant.
Connect with the butterflies and absorb the Vitamin D. This will boost
the serotonin levels, which is a feel-good neurotransmitter. You would
also need to increase the neurotransmitters dopamine, nor epinephrine
and adrenaline. These control motivation and drive. For this to happen,
your body needs folic acid, magnesium, zinc and copper. You'll find them
in nuts, whole grain cereals, pulses, leafy greens, aubergine, and french
beans, sprouts and okra. You'll also benefit from fish or fish oil capsules.
The advantages of this regime will be that your blood sugar will also be
regulated.

5) <u>Dr PK's Holistic Medico Advisory</u> shared <u>Hawaii GMO Justice Coalition's</u> <u>photo</u>.

This info if put into practice can change your health structure for the better in a few weeks.
When I started on it by eating guavas, oranges and grapes, my body suddenly became active and for a few days phlegm was thrown out like mad. And after that came relief from continuous sneezes, breathing problems, gastric burning and more tolerance of strong smells and dusty places.

THIS IS THE MOST IMPORTANT CHART YOU WILL EVER LOOK AT!

Learn about alkaline vs. acidic foods.

Cancer, parasites and most diseases grows in acidic environments.

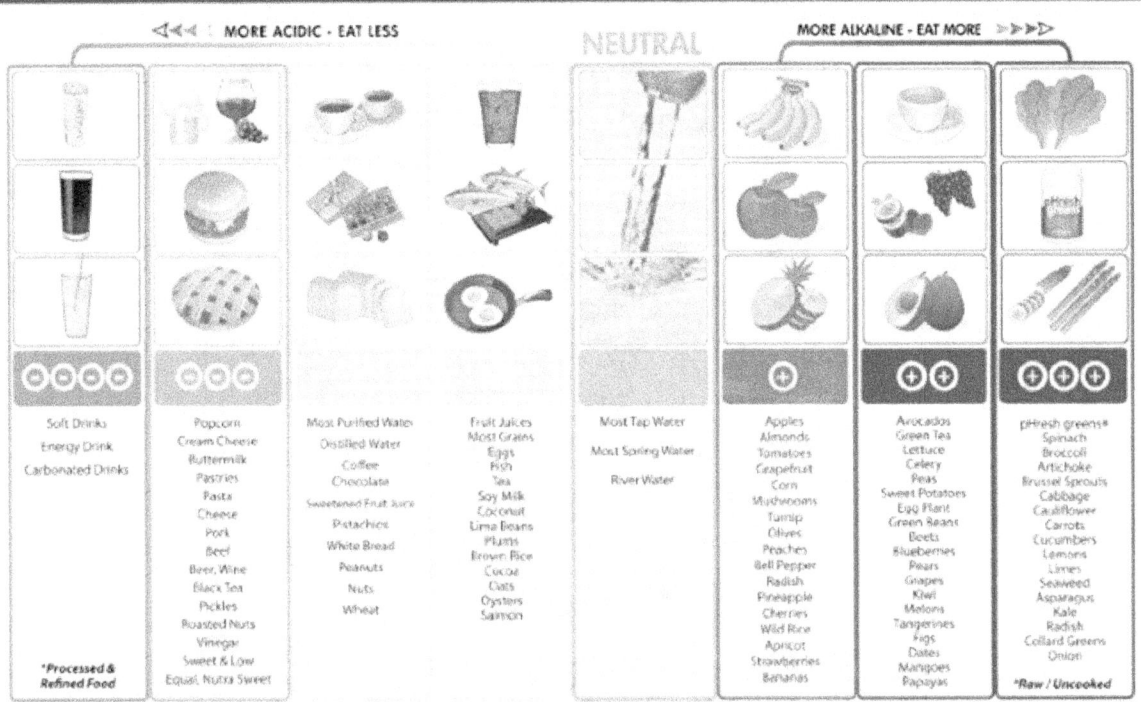

6) Dr PK's Holistic Medico Advisory shared
Stay Healthy fitness's photo.   January 11

I would advise this regimen but don't blame me if you don't find pesticide-free and properly grown stuff.
DETOX YOUR BODY!!! Check out this fabulous list of super foods to naturally cleanse the body. No pills or drinks required. Stay Healthy~

 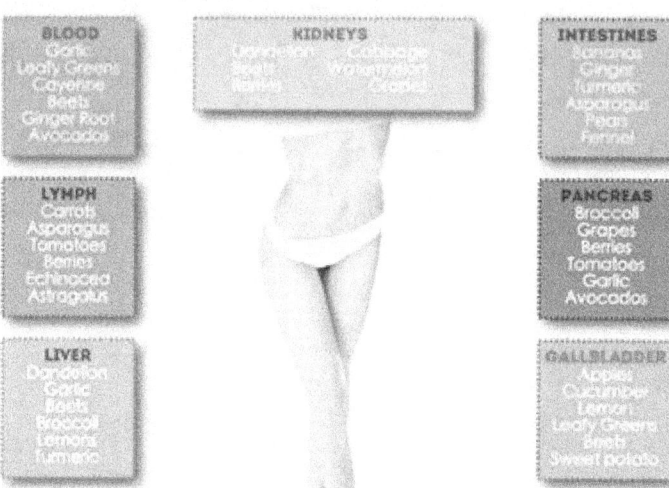

DETOX Your BODY

LIVE LOVE FRUIT

WWW.LIVELOVEFRUIT.COM

BLOOD
Garlic
Leafy Greens
Cayenne
Beets
Ginger Root
Avocados

KIDNEYS
Dandelion   Cabbage
Beets   Watermelon
Nettle   Grapes

INTESTINES
Bananas
Ginger
Turmeric
Asparagus
Pears
Fennel

LYMPH
Carrots
Asparagus
Tomatoes
Berries
Echinacea
Astragalus

PANCREAS
Broccoli
Grapes
Berries
Tomatoes
Garlic
Avocados

LIVER
Dandelion
Garlic
Beets
Broccoli
Lemons
Turmeric

GALLBLADDER
Apples
Cucumber
Lemon
Leafy Greens
Beets
Sweet potato

7)   A conversation worth noting.

From a concerned mother..
What do you recommend for a child with croupy cough and sob swollen throat pretty sudden onset
Gave Homoeopathic Hepar sulph, Aconite & Belladonna
Improved a bit immediately. Also my herbal syrup of 25 different herbs. After 10 min gap.

Ok it's hard to treat own; we worry and second guess.
Just don't want to take to dr and have steroids given
Dr Pk
Seems Ok to me. You can also give chicken soup. And hot orange juice with honey
You can also give your herbal syrup in fairly warm water one cup or so every 2 hours.
Concerned mother..
Using hyssop and eucalyptus radiata essential oils
Oh yes I will make stock
He did have orange today it's his favorite
Organic whole oranges though.
Some say orange creates mucus?
Dr Pk
People think of oranges as acidic. Not true.
Juice and soup is required. Colds, blocked sinus happen only when the system/liver is suffering from overload, specially in the colon and negative flora has gone out of control.
Concerned mother..
I agree he tends to crave sugars
I don't keep in house but others give him lollipop etc
Dr Pk
Had the same problem with my daughter, then put my foot down - stopped people - they like it or not
Concerned mother..
Yes I get very angry. Why do ppl equate sugar with love...?!
Dr Pk
Getting angry is not the solution. DO!
Concerned mother..
It is nice to be reassured
Dr Pk
Yes. Definitely

8) Dr PK's Holistic Medico Advisory

Fear; not "Joy" is our motivation.

People are afraid to sleep on the grass for fear of bugs, walk in the rain afraid to catch a chill, sanitation stops them from going out into the open where toilets and toilet paper are not available, scared to fall asleep for fear of being robbed, afraid of drinking water from a stream

because of pollution and confront the dew in the morning and tragically avoid going bare-foot for fear of pebbles and sharp protrusions.
What ninnies we have become.
All looks well. The figure is right. The shape and stand is perfect even better than it used to be. It looks no different than that of any aborigine in the woods. Yet it knows very well that it has lost a lot of its natural strength, its resistance to natural phenomena without and immunity to sickness attacks within.
But is it bothered? Not one bit. Its confidence in modern techno-based medicine is supreme. When I look at modern man and his apparent health, I am amazed at the ability of man to ignore the monster standing right in front of his eyes.
It has become something like a fully armed, in-full-gear-modern soldier but with no bullets or any kind of ammunition.
Good only for a photo-shoot.

9) Dr PK's Holistic Medico Advisory

How we create adults who will be sick tomorrow -

When we shower our child with constructive criticism (mostly with anger in our being), are we really "bettering" him or battering him and taking out our frustration and fatigue out on him?

Be careful of the words you use. Too much of it will only make him cry and kill his will to live. This will in turn make him not study or eat properly. It will start a trend towards bad mental and physical health. Being a parent is tantamount to being the parent of this Mother earth because the child will carry forth all that you have instilled in him today.

So be kind, try to understand and explain to the child the ways of the world in a language he can sense of.
Be gentle and help he child to explore and understand.

Your words today...will become her inner voice... forever.
~z2z~

10) **Dr PK's Holistic Medico Advisory** shared The Cornucopia Institute's photo.

This is a fact and needs to be taken into our calculations of nutrition, diet and eating habits.
My experience is that it is virtually difficult/impossible to manage without supplements.

Every single individual without exception is suffering from some deficiency or other and illness or/and minor aches and pains directly related to it.

Fruits and vegetables grown decades ago were much richer in vitamins and minerals than the varieties most of us get today. The main culprit in this disturbing nutritional trend is soil depletion: Modern intensive agricultural methods have stripped increasing amounts of nutrients from the soil in which the food we eat grows. The solution is to purchase local, organic food from farmers that value their soil.

Source links for information:
Symphony of the Soil http://vimeo.com/64662202
University of Texas paper:
http://www.utexas.edu/news/2004/12/01/nr_chemistry

https://www.cncahealth.com/explore/learn/nutrition-food/declining-nutrition-of-fruits-and-vegetables#.Upy-x5Q4Vr0

http://www.nationofchange.org/nutritional-value-food-risk-fruits-and-vegetables-now-less-nutritious-1355070081

http://www.scientificamerican.com/article.cfm?id=soil-depletion-and-nutrition-loss

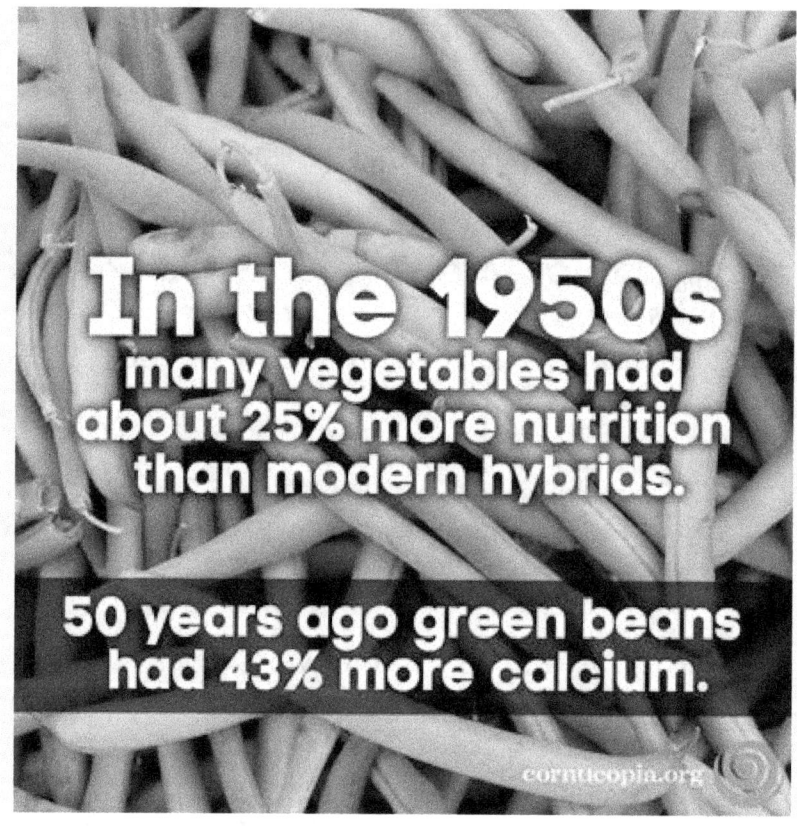

11) A Prescription worth its weight in gold.

- 2 spoons of bran in one cup of yoghurt. Best taken before the meal at least once a day.

The milling of wheat and rice takes away the nutritious bran which contains the essential vitamins and minerals + roughage. About 150 years ago, we were meeting our entire vitamin E requirement through un-milled grains. This has now come down to only about 10%. No wonder we are sick because all the other oil based vitamins also do not get properly absorbed or utilized, including Vit D.

Yogurt is nutritionally rich in protein, calcium, riboflavin, vitamin B6 and vitamin B12.

Yogurt is a valuable health food for both infants and elderly persons. For children, it is a balanced source of protein, fats, carbohydrates, and minerals. For senior citizens, who usually have more sensitive colons or whose intestines have run out of lactase, yogurt is also a valuable food. Elderly intestines showed declining levels of bifidus bacteria, which allow the growth of toxin-producing and, perhaps, cancer-causing bacteria. Yogurt may help prevent osteoporosis, reduce the risk of high blood pressure. Yogurt with active cultures helps the gut, may discourage vaginal infections, and may help one feel fuller.

LASSI – yoghurt drink.

It is made by mixing yogurt with water and salt or sugar. The same drink is known as *doogh* in Iran; *tan* in Armenia; *laban ayran* in Syria and Lebanon; *shenina* in Iraq and Jordan; *laban arbil* in Iraq; namkeen *lassi* in north India and all over Pakistan.
This salty drink is popular in Iran, Albania, Bulgaria, Turkey, Azerbaijan, Afghanistan, Pakistan, Bangladesh, the Republic of Macedonia, Kazakhstan and Kyrgyzstan.

RAITA (3rd photo)

This is yoghurt stirred with chopped herbs like mint or vegetables and fruits pieces - it can be salted or sugared.

Worldwide, cow's milk, the protein of which mainly comprises casein, is most commonly used to make yogurt, but milk from water buffalo, goats, ewes, mares, camels, and yaks is also used in various parts of the world.

Dairy yogurt is produced using a culture of _Lactobacillus delbrueckii_ subsp. _bulgaricus_ and _Streptococcus thermophilus_ bacteria. In addition, other lactobacilli and bifidobacteria are also sometimes added during or after culturing yogurt.

12) These environmental factors have to be taken seriously.

Air pollution has increased dirt in lungs and this lowers immunity resulting in breathing problems, sinus problems, running noses and eyes with itching, skin allergies and sore throats etc which if not stopped right there, become more complex illnesses as the infection spreads and grows in the body.

Similarly the water is polluted and the food items are not pure. This creates a toxic overload on the digestive system, specially the liver. This results in gastric re-flux, acidity, nausea, discomfort, traveling sickness etc.

Homeopathically these symptoms can be stopped if medication is started as soon as noticed.
If you are not sure what to do, please feel free to contact me.

13) <u>Dr PK's Holistic Medico Advisory</u> shared <u>Dr. Fibro's</u>photo.

(Trade names include: Sweet-N-Low, Equal and Splenda.) DO NOT allow the product into your home if it contains those things. Be especially alert when the packaging says "diet", "light", "0 calories" or "no sugar added" or "sugar free"- as these products are often loaded with these and other chemicals.

Most of you probably already know this, but... most artificial sweeteners cause auto-immune response effects which can increase inflammation around the body and therefore, worsen Fibro symptoms.

Easily the #1 thing you must cut from your diet completely - if you haven't already - is artificial sweeteners.

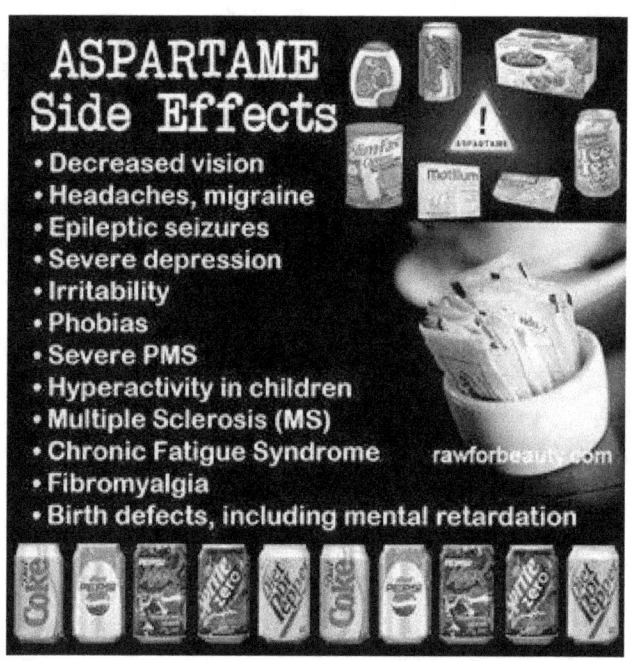

READ PRODUCT LABELS FOR: Aspartame, neotame, sucralose, saccharin, acesulfame. (Trade names include: Sweet-N-Low, Equal and Splenda.)

14) Dr PK's Holistic Medico Advisory

If you read older treaties by philosophers like Rochefoucauld, Francis Bacon and others, you will see that they had a very deep understanding of the emotional miasms affecting the body. The entire understanding of medical help was based mainly on it.
It is time we went back to understand that all the three - thoughts, emotions and bodily functions depend and affect each other.

Let us discuss and teach each other what we know.

15) Dr PK's Holistic Medico Advisory shared Ayurveda'sphoto.

Spinach - food as medicine.

Spinach is cool, mild, relishing, causes the formation of urine. It activates the intestine. It is also beneficial in the diseases and eliminates the excessive bile in the body. It also eliminates the excessive formation of bile and phlegm in the body, purifies the blood. It cures stone and strengthens the bone. Vegetable prepared from spinach leaves gives strength and keeps away diseases. The juice extracted from the leaves of spinach melts the stones formed in the kidney and the fragmented stones come out through urine.

http://curejoy.com/content/

Spinach has one negative side and that is its iron content which can unbalance the vitamin E levels and those already deficient in Vit E it may have adverse symptoms to report.
In India, specially in the rainy season, we also like to dip the leaves in batter made from chickpeas flour and then deep fry. This we do also with potatoes, onion slices and aubergine, cauliflower, chilies and what not.

What is Spinach Good For?

www.curejoy.com ~ Expert Advice on Alternative Cure, Fitness & Beauty

Though the deep frying is really not good, specially in poor quality oils at the very high temperatures because the batter absorbs a lot of oil and can be difficult on the digestion.

16) <u>Dr PK's Holistic Medico Advisory</u> shared <u>Vegiheal.com</u>'s <u>photo</u>.

It is all there and we are busy destroying the eco-system in our shortsightedness.
In India these elements have always been in use and advised by grandmothers.
Our Chyawanprash is based on Gooseberry, saffron and spices and has been used as an immunity builder since thousands of years.

Health Benefits of Pomegranate

Fights Breast Cancer
Studies in Israel show that pomegranate juice destroys breast cancer cells while leaving healthy cells alone. It may also prevent breast cancer cells from forming.
Lung Cancer Prevention
Studies in mice show that pomegranate juice may inhibit the development of lung cancer.
Slows Prostate Cancer
It slowed the growth of prostate cancer in mice. Keeps PSA Levels Stable In a study of 50 men who had undergone treatment for prostate cancer, 8 ounces of pomegranate juice per day kept PSA levels stable, reducing the need for further treatment such as chemotherapy or hormone therapy.
Protects the Neonatal Brain
Studies show that maternal consumption of pomegranate juice may protect the neonatal brain from damage after injury.
Prevention of Osteoarthritis
Several studies indicate that pomegranate juice may prevent cartilage deterioration.

Protects the Arteries. It prevents plaque from building up in the arteries and may reverse previous plaque buildup.
Alzheimer's Disease Prevention: It may prevent and slow Alzheimer's disease.
It lowers LDL (bad cholesterol) and raises HDL (good cholesterol).
Lowers Blood Pressure
One study showed that drinking 1.7 ounces of pomegranate juice per day lowered systolic blood pressure by as much as 5 percent.
Dental Protection
Research suggests that drinking pomegranate juice may be a natural way to prevent dental plaque.

17) <u>Dr PK's Holistic Medico Advisory</u> shared <u>Karmin's</u><u>photo</u>.

Music is highly therapeutic.

Modern medicine developed in the west and the search there for natural de-stressors have led the researchers to music. Something that in India has been well understood and known but now there is the scientific method to back up what we understood empirically.

It is becoming clear that the thalamus – the nerve center of all our moods and feelings and responses, including that of pain is awfully influenced by the rhythms of perfectly metered sounds. In the Indian way of life we have Vedic chants and in classical music, perfectly formulated and balanced raags.

The Vedic chants are old and tried formulas that have the power to create vibrations of a very powerful nature and an occult strength that has an inherent creative seed. The raags are also very scientific; and specific raags have definite and pertinent effects on the nervous system. When the thalamus is vibrating happily, it gets the brain's cortex dancing as well.

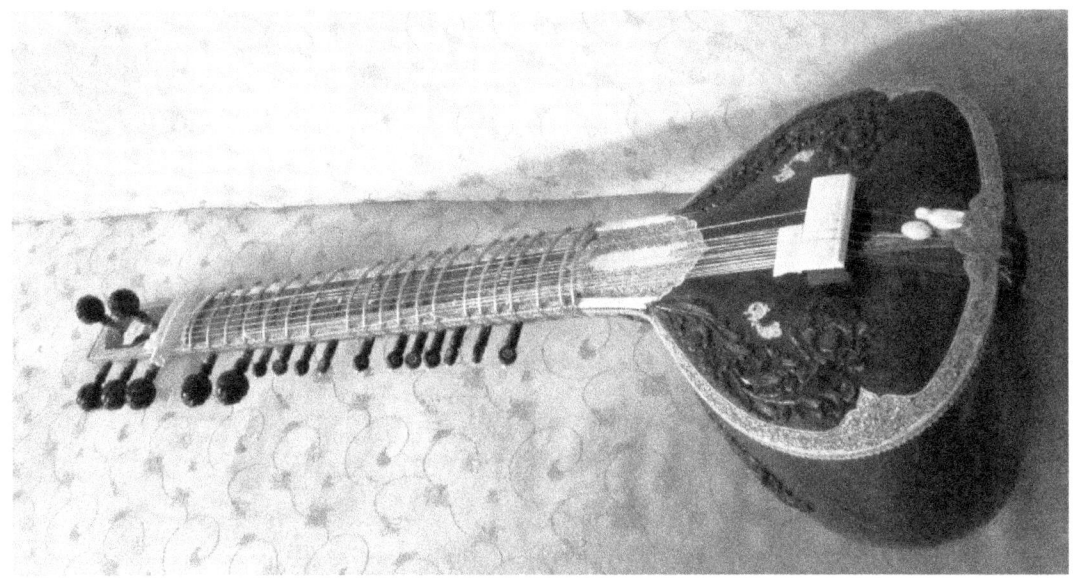

A sitar.

This has a correlating influence on our feelings and thoughts directly. The positive vibrations can stimulate healing at the basic level where the whole body metabolism defies medical knowledge of today and effectively goes into a self-healing mode. Let's hear it

18) Dr PK's Holistic Medico Advisory

Better safe than sorry. What have they done to our world?! And we let it happen - that is the tragedy.
Good to know, especially with so many insecticides and other poisons contaminating our foods today.
Learn how to wash and remove the pesticides from fruits and vegetables by washing scrubbing in running water before using them.

19) Dr PK's Holistic Medico Advisory

Stress? What stress?

I become my child's companion, listen to music, paint, read an enthralling spy novel, do exactly as my wife tells me to and take naps. We can reduce our stress by cutting out all that can be cut out. Learn to ignore. Running the world is not our responsibility.

Go back to the child in you. Don't be afraid to make a fool of yourself. Don't overdo and kill yourself but also don't just sit there. It will kill you anyway.

Go for all the small things that give you contentment; Friends and activities. Create a small impenetrable corner where you can be yourself. Let the world go to Jericho if it wants to. Do your best and sleep well after a day well spent.

20)   **Dr PK's Holistic Medico Advisory** shared a link.

Homeopathy along with correct diet can be wonderfully effective in keeping us away from major sicknesses.

Find a Remedy | National Center for Homeopathy

homeopathycenter.org

It's easy to get started using homeopathy at home. You don't need to be an expert in anatomy, physiology, or pharmacology. You only need to be able to observe your and your family's symptoms and any changes you might see in those symptoms.

21)   Massage.

Massage as treatment is very good for the body. It helps to alleviate conditions due to inactivity by artificially forcing activity. This results in the entire organs, blood circulation and he metabolism to wake up and do their thing more willingly.

A full body massage can be very rejuvenating.

Similarly other arts of Acupressure and Reflexology, Shiatsu etc are simple to learn and put into practice.

When you know the points to massage to activate certain regions or organs, the relief obtained is dramatic.

Here is an easy to understand chart for reflexology points in the feet.

To study more, there is a lot of detailed information on the internet.

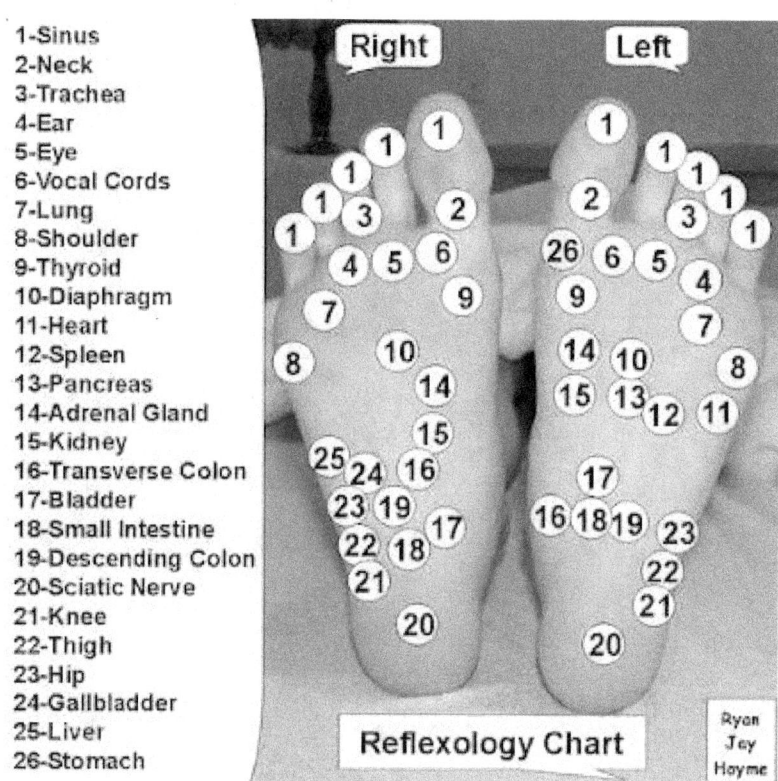

1-Sinus
2-Neck
3-Trachea
4-Ear
5-Eye
6-Vocal Cords
7-Lung
8-Shoulder
9-Thyroid
10-Diaphragm
11-Heart
12-Spleen
13-Pancreas
14-Adrenal Gland
15-Kidney
16-Transverse Colon
17-Bladder
18-Small Intestine
19-Descending Colon
20-Sciatic Nerve
21-Knee
22-Thigh
23-Hip
24-Gallbladder
25-Liver
26-Stomach

Reflexology Chart

22) Dr PK's Holistic Medico Advisory

The lack of our interest to go out in the open is making us seriously deficient in Vit D. I attribute this to the fear of discomfort from heat, dust and sweat. All these promotions for antiperspirants, deodorants, sun-blocks and deliberate scaring by the medical fraternity against skin cancer have driven people indoors.

Lack of Vit D creates a chain reaction that stops many other nutrients (vitamins and minerals) to NOT be absorbed at all.

Treat going out as medicinal. It helps your body, your eyes as they get some opportunity to focus on infinity, and helps the mind to distend.

Sunshine is free and available. But most prefer the air conditioned interior of their "managed" environment.

And what happens when power goes out?
That is the unthinkable, un-thought and not to be thought of part.

23) SLEEP. MY KINGDOM FOR SOME SLEEP.

What would be rated as the most prevalent disease today? Sleep Deprivation! Something as natural as sleep not coming by is a daunting thought. How can this be a problem? Look at the newborn sleeping away his whole day. The world is today a planet of troubled sleepers. Where and what happened to them?

People have so revamped their lives that they are simply not able to fall asleep easily. It has now reached a serious problem status.

There are over 200 000 road-deaths all over the world per year due to the inability or not being able to have a full night's proper rest.

Sleep deficit hurts directly the individual and the social group one moves in. Health-wise it ends by depressing the immune system, which opens the door to a plethora of diseases, and emotionally it depresses you quite literally. Coordination becomes weak and shaky. Accidents and error of judgments at all levels of life occur.

24) My observations from life on how we miss certain factors that slide us toward ill health.

1) There seems to be a tendency which seems a little of that macho arrogance that we can tolerate bad weather better than others. People refuse to accept the seriousness of chilly weather or severe hot weather. They feel that physically they are so much stronger (and visibly grander) than all the sickly humans around them. The viral fever attacks, other fevers like rheumatism etc that are now seen around us are due to this fact of ignoring the acute effect these cold and heat conditions have on our immunity which sort of gets hit by an avalanche and goes under.

2) Then we deliberately ignore that we now live rather protected lives – protected from the extremes of the weather. Our resistances and immunity are no more tuned to the hardships that our forefathers were tuned for. Additionally our environment is more stressful and our bodies are already under great stress from the working needs, polluted conditions and things like more noise and less sleep. We need to really be more open & aware to the idea that we are more fallible than generations before us and that we now have so much more to protect us with that we should put to good use and that taking chances is not a good idea.

3) People are unnecessarily pushing themselves into conditions of sickness. Take for instance diabetes. We are rationalising this illness in many ways whereas the simple truth is that by breaking simple rules of the body we are bringing it upon us. We go hungry for long periods, letting sugar level go way down then suddenly overload the body with sugary/high-carb foods which throws the pancreas into an unnatural tizzy state to regulate the sugar load and it goes into producing insulin – a total confused state. This see-saw of low sugar, then too much sugar and then too much insulin which the rest of the body then helps to level off is too much of a burden which eventually brings about a collapse.

4) If you value your heath, please eat regularly and make it always a balanced platter. Don't let the blood sugar level go down too much. Take a healthy snack or sandwich.

5) Women do no pay attention to the fact that they are losing a huge amount of valuable essential vitamins & minerals for most of their lives and these are never fully replaced. They need to really counter this loss properly by taking their diet and supplements seriously. The losses create anaemic conditions and shortages of Vitamins D, C, E calcium etc. This reduces their blood oxygen, strains the nerves and gives rise to back pain, sciatica problems, headaches and regular sense of fatigue which is very real.

6) Another important fact that is going against all naturopathic principles is that we are delaying listening to the calls of nature. This should not be allowed.

7) Men need to worry a little about their sex drives. Prostate problems are growing because there is sex on the mind but no outlet physically. Often people get excited and the semen gets fully loaded but the urge is not satisfied due to circumstances. This semen is absorbed back into the body with difficulty and many men feel acute pain too. In many it create infectious conditions. So learn to throw his semen out or learn to calm your mind.

8) Most people are living around with exhausted adrenals. No wonder steroid medications have become so important a tool in modern medicine. The onus of our health is on us. There are good preparations to boost our vitality and keep the adrenals in a good state. Even regular multivitamin supplements help. They should be taken as supplements as buffers before the body slips into a disease state.

25) Dr Pk (in response to point raised below)

It is simply a matter of going back to nature to maintain a healthy balance, giving the body all the ammunition it needs to fight off sickness on its own.
No herb, fruits vegetable or food is single-handedly a magic bullet.

This is the false active ingredient approach of modern medicine backed by intensive media support's brain-washing.
The tragedy is in the fact that even people who think "nature" are affected.

Edward Stanulevich IV :
The thing with a lot of these herbs and plants is that they work great in a

test tube but they don't always help in a live patient. When you eat your food, the compounds in it are altered by digestion. Too often, the concentration of the active ingredients needed for good effect is too high for you to be able to eat enough of it for it to work.

26) Our guts are a very intelligent and sensitive to the emotions and thoughts that we are generating continuously in us. The joys and fears affect directly our entire glandular and digestive system which finally controls our health.

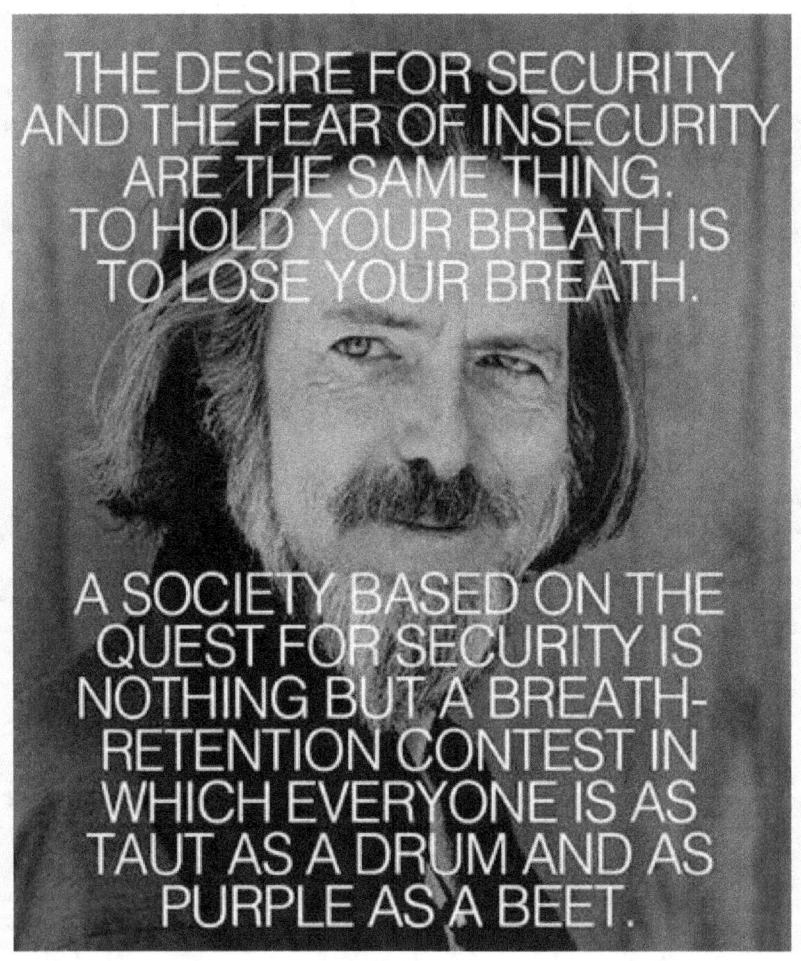

THE DESIRE FOR SECURITY AND THE FEAR OF INSECURITY ARE THE SAME THING. TO HOLD YOUR BREATH IS TO LOSE YOUR BREATH.

A SOCIETY BASED ON THE QUEST FOR SECURITY IS NOTHING BUT A BREATH-RETENTION CONTEST IN WHICH EVERYONE IS AS TAUT AS A DRUM AND AS PURPLE AS A BEET.

99% of our activities in pursuit of major goals of life are aimed to achieve security from the vagaries of life. Obviously we must be a very insecure lot and therefore I can safely assume - a sickly lot!

27) Dr PK's Holistic Medico Advisory

This book changed the way I interacted with life. It made all the difference and put me on the way to better health. From it I learnt how

vitamins and minerals work. How we are destroying them in the processing and cooking of food. How erroneous practices have been adopted that are actually doing harm in the guise of better products.

28) <u>Dr PK's Holistic Medico Advisory</u>

A healthy gut is life-giving and the source of good health.
Probiotic bacteria may have the potential to alter brain neurochemistry, affecting anxiety and depression-related disorders.
The study, published in the Proceedings of the National Academy of Sciences, demonstrated that mice fed with Lactobacillus rhamnosus JB-1 showed significantly fewer stress, anxiety and depression-related behaviors than those fed with just broth. + lower levels of the stress-induced hormone, corticosterone.
"These findings highlight the important role that gut bacteria play in the bidirectional communication between the gut and the brain, the gut–brain axis.

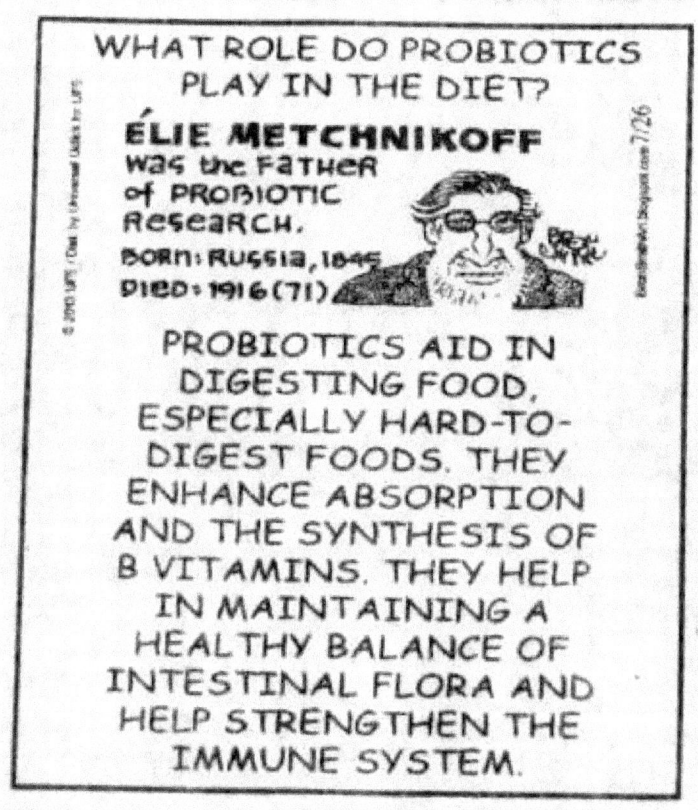

29) Dr PK's Holistic Medico Advisory

Snoring.

Can we get rid of snoring? There doesn't seem to be much we can do about it. But if made aware of it, I think we should try out a few things like I for one sleep at an incline - I prefer a recliner sofa. I also think that nutrients like Vit D, Calcium, E and good cholesterol could well be deficient in the snorer and would have been so for a very long time, it is I assume because of this that the vocal cords and wind-pipe harden and loose their flexibility so then work like a horn.

30) Dr PK's Holistic Medico Advisory (**from Yahoo**)

Tooth decay. The real causes.
Until recently it was believed that tooth decay is caused by sugars and starches that remain on the teeth. But studies on indigenous people who do not brush or floss show that many have teeth almost completely free of tooth decay.

Research conducted by Dr. Westom Price and other dental pioneers suggest that the real cause of tooth decay is:
Lack of minerals in the diet.

Lack of fat-soluble vitamins (A,D,E & K)
A weak not well provided or maintained Intestinal system, unable to properly absorb nutrients
Presence of phytic acid (from grains, seeds, nuts, and legumes)
Over time, the blood chemistry and ratio of calcium and phosphorous become disproportionate and result in minerals being removed from the bones, causing bone and tooth decay. In order to restore balance to the body and enable minerals to bond to our teeth, it is important to consume a diet rich in minerals and vitamins. This will build a hard glassy tooth structure.
Foods to include are:

Coconut oil, organic dairy (butter), organic meats, seafood and bone broths.
Organic vegetables
Organ and gland meats (like liver)
Limit intake of processed food like flours and sugars that de-stabilise blood sugar balance

31) Dr PK's Holistic Medico Advisory

The importance of sleep. How we shortchange ourselves when we deprive ourselves of it

Brain gets rid of toxins as we sleep

Kounteya Sinha | TNN

London: It's a wake-up call for an estimated 150 million people who don't get enough sleep. Scientists say sleep is the mechanism through which the body flushes waste from the human brain.

The brain's method of waste removal — the glymphatic system — is highly active during sleep, clearing away toxins responsible for Alzheimer's disease and other neurological disorders, according to a study.

Researchers say the brain's cells reduce in size during sleep, allowing waste to be removed more effectively. "This study shows that the brain has different functional states when asleep and when awake," said Maiken Nedergaard of the University of Rochester Medical Centre. "In fact, the restorative nature of sleep appears to be the

32) Dr PK's Holistic Medico Advisory

Power pack Stuffed Beetroot, Radish and Carrot Paratha (Sauted Indian bread)
This paratha is a simple and easy recipe, and is packed with nutrients, fibre and potassium. It is made by using root vegetables (beetroot, radish and carrot), which are rich in nutrients, low in fat & calories. (**Yahoo**).

33) <u>Dr PK's Holistic Medico Advisory</u>

I am a great believer in the goodness of Pineapples. We buy ours from the local weekly market which is then peeled and sliced in front of us. We then steam them at home. Nothing helps the system clear itself out and make us feel lighter like this fruit does. I can ardently recommend one dinner per week of pineapple only to help stabilize the performance of the colon.

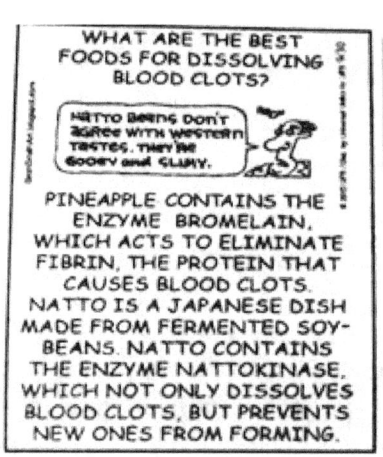

34)   Dr PK's Holistic Medico Advisory

Try these combos out. They are great and have proven remedial rejuvenating actions. Just be vary of doing too much of it on the principle that if some is good, more is better. It never is. And, if you listen to your body, the body will help you select and work out your own combos depending on the fruits available locally wherever you are and in season.

HEALTHY JUICES FOR TOTAL WELLNESS:-

Recommend below are the secret recipe for healthy drinking.

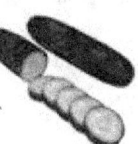

Carrot + Ginger + Apple
> Boost and cleanse our system.

Apple + Cucumber + Celery
> Prevent cancer, reduce cholesterol, and improve stomach upset and headache.

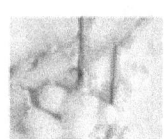

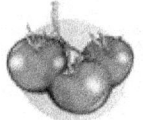

Tomato + Carrot + Apple
> Improve skin complexion and bad breath.

Bitter gourd + Apple + Milk
> Avoid bad breath and reduce internal body heat.

Orange + Ginger + Cucumber
> Improve skin texture and moisture and reduce body heat.

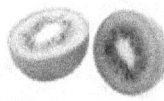

Pineapple + Apple + Watermelon
> To dispel excess salts, nourishes the bladder and kidney

Apple + Cucumber + Kiwi
> To improves skin complexion.

Pear & Banana
> To regulates sugar content.

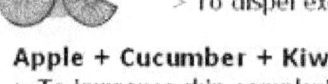

Carrot + Apple + Pear + Mango
> Clear body heat, counteracts toxicity, decreased blood pressure and Fight oxidization!

Honeydew + Grape + Watermelon + Milk
> Rich in vitamin C + Vitamin B2 that increases cell activity and Strengthen body immunity.

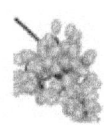

Papaya + Pineapple + Milk
> Rich in vitamin C, E, Iron. Improve skin complexion and metabolism.

Banana + Pineapple + Milk
> Rich in Vitamin with nutritious and prevent constipation

36) Dr PK's Holistic Medico Advisory

To follow the circadian rhythm, eat when the body signals hunger and sleep when sleepy. The first lesson of Zen is when hungry eat, when sleepy, sleep. We tend to brush aside the body's signals to accommodate our other requisites. The mind can and does over-ride the body's signals and it forces the body to go along with its wishes that are in turn being imposed by the desire-center. etc etc etc. The body pays or all this. We just need to pay attention to the body's signals and we shall know for sure. Never fight the inclinations to rest, or needing sustenance when your sugar levels, fatigue levels and other aches & stresses demand.

37) Dr PK's Holistic Medico Advisory

You can trust me totally on this:

Medicines work best with fasting to help the body get rid of toxins by taking a liquid diet for 2-3 days. In this I recommend Buttermilk, Natural lemonade, Barley water, a light nourishing drink like Horlicks. Normal water with mint drops (in India available as Pudinhara). Occasional green tea or light coffee is also permissible.

The body and spirit feel lighter and more alive. Contentment in the daytime and good sleep at night become regular friends.

Air pollution has increased dirt in lungs and this lowers immunity resulting in breathing problems, sinus problems, running noses and eyes with itching, skin allergies and sore throats etc which if not stopped right there, become more complex illnesses as the infection spreads and grows in the body. Similarly the water is polluted and the food items are not pure. This creates a toxic overload on the digestive system, specially the liver. This results in gastric reflux, acidity, nausea, discomfort, traveling sickness etc.

My own family is proof of the effectivity of the above regimen.

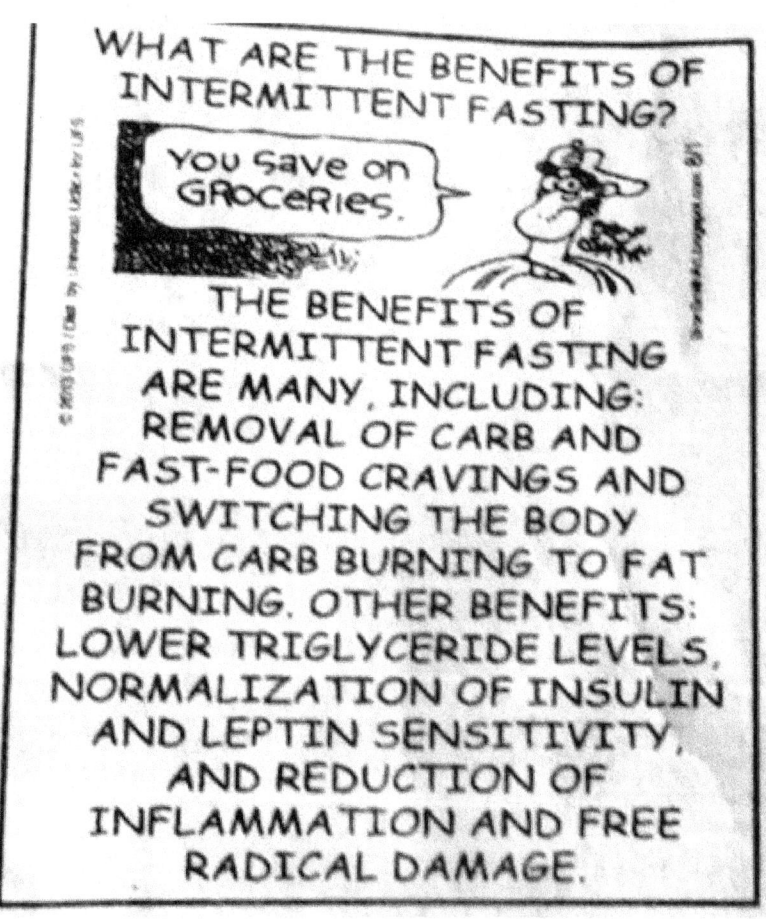

38) <u>Dr PK's Holistic Medico Advisory</u> shared <u>Historic Images</u>'s <u>photo</u>.

Fresh and sunlight are the first main ingredients for growing up in a well balanced whole person.
Baby cages used to ensure that children get enough sunlight and fresh air when living in an apartment building, ca. 1937. Quite fascinating really!

Today's tragedy is that we are afraid of sunlight and as our bodies are less able to tolerate stress, the effect of sunlight quickly gives sun-burns or sun-strokes. It's a travesty that sun lamps are used for tanning!

39) <u>Dr PK's Holistic Medico Advisory</u> shared <u>Stay Healthy Fitness</u>'s <u>photo</u>.

WHY I EAT BUTTER!

Don't be afraid. It won't hurt you. Just think. This is a product that has been eaten and used in cooking since the last history can remember and suddenly it has become dangerous stuff. It is the media that has created this scare on some idiotic assumptions by the still evolving research in food things. Medically this ghost has now been laid to rest. Eat as much as you want. You can't eat more than your body can take in. Can you?

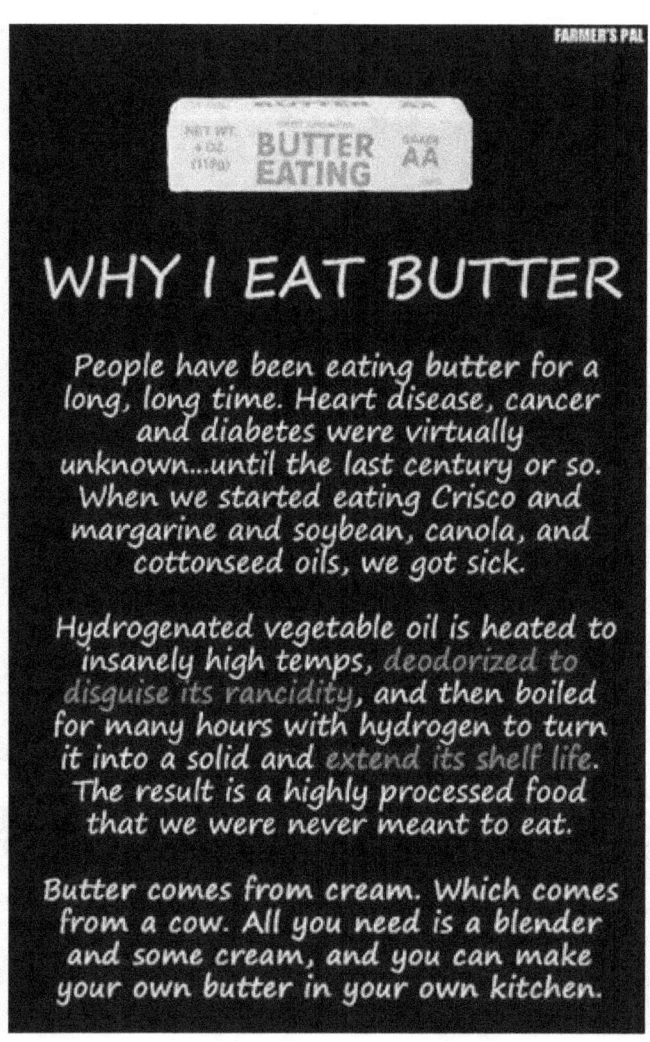

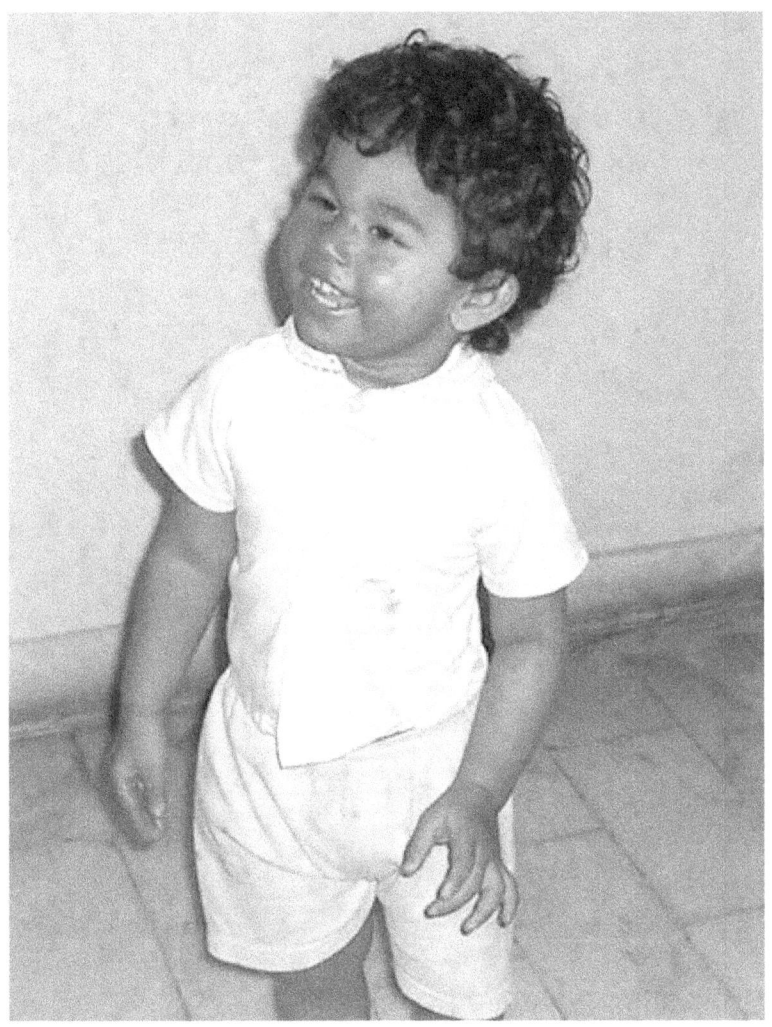

Find your own fount of happiness.
One has to understand the process and adapt our own personal tendencies with the life we are born in and the facilities available to us. Following regimens by the book are always dangerous.
One has to balance with what is with what should be and can be.
Indications and information are there to minimize noxious effects, not to sanitise life by following rigid rules applicable in all circumstances.

"For example: Not worrying too much about the clothes your child is wearing because you have lazily rationalized that this will increase the natural resistance of the body." This is precisely what has happened to a 3 month's old unwanted baby to some working class/uneducated people I know. The baby is dead from pneumonia. Now they are blaming fate and doctors.

What rubbish.

You cannot forsake "thinking" but if you are so inclined, please do not place the blame at other's doorstep as we normally do when things don't go right.

41) **Dr PK's Holistic Medico Advisory** shared <u>True African Art.com</u>'s <u>photo</u>.

The first thing I noticed was the head-rest.

I have been paying a lot of attention to headrests since my childhood. I noticed the versions used since early Egyptian times, in other cultures and all.

Such an important equipment and most people do not take it seriously. They compromise on it and suffer for it gladly. Too lazy to listen to their bodies and do something about it.

A pillow is something we use for more than one third of the time of our whole life. If you calculate, it is the longest time duration involved in use of any equipment in our lives.

Head rest, is it comfortable? Africans say yes.

42) Dr PK's Holistic Medico Advisory

The microbes/virus/cancer and such theory and its devastating action in treatment of illnesses.

Why do people call it a battle? Are we treating them or going to war? The microbes are designed by Nature do a job. If you let them, they will do their thing. First we create the best possible environment for them to proliferate and then we fight them without improving or correcting the environment which has now become their space. The modern mind has devised some horrific systems to fight them. This destroys the invader and the castle. It is like throwing the baby with the bath water.

Then we complain that the battle was lost.

The body has a simple memory system that records everything (please note that I am NOT talking of the mental memory but a subliminal memory of the body which is an entirely different thing).

Too many activities at the same time or in speedy succession can confuse it and deregulate its memory and cause stress. This is the basic reason behind advising - to eat simple fare and not too many things at a time - not having too many partners – to be engaged in too many complex projects.

This causes stress and as the mind is directly involved the mind also gets derailed. You go nuts - no specific reason needed to be identified or required (the modern medicine doctors and pharma are cashing on this). This is basically behind the anxiety levels, depression levels, sense of insecurity and stress induced illnesses of today's multi-faceted electronic culture. Think of the body as slow computer with a very simple operating program - like the computers of was 1980s or so at best.

Our older cultures that were closer or are closer to nature, reflect and practice this understanding. Even Homoeopathy is very near to this understanding - it depends on the memory contained in the physical-material envelop of the earth to activate the healing process.

Unfortunately, people are not interested. Humans do not see - do not want to see - the connection in the long term effects of most activities. Habits and immediate pleasures are the prime motivators.

I am studying this subject of change in diet and food habits constantly. Ayurveda our traditional medicine of India understood these subtleties and through rituals made correct living part of our way of life in India.

43) Dr PK's Holistic Medico Advisory shared Modest Needs Foundation's photo.

Have you ever considered or given thought to the fact that your attitudes often are behind your ailments?
At the individual level, there is an inherent need to progress and go further on the evolutionary scale. But given the mental capacity and character endowed to us by Mother Nature we have only a limited scope for movement. Then to this, Destiny adds elements like the limitations of

the environment as controlled by parents, elders, teachers, family, friends and opportunities etc. By the time a young man is ready to launch himself in life some parameters and choices are already set as imposed by life with only limited options if any; such as the general goal to earn a living and then have a family which is equated with happiness. Of course the individual at a younger age can't see many other options and perforce finds himself in a cyclic flow of things rarely in his control. The ego and vanities also play a very big part. With age parameters change and the choices diminish even further.

Soon the individual finds himself trapped, frustrated and depressed. He is left adjusting to everybody around him who has even the slightest power to disrupt his life and is incessantly in the compromising mode. Keeping the status quo becomes the main effort in life. The life around is constantly rearranging itself while the individual fights to maintain his place in the order of things. The ego asks for its penny worth and is forever complicating the situation. This creates an anomaly of gigantic proportions which only grows bigger with time.

So where is the solution? The solution is in the understanding that life is a creative process and this process is always on and is flowing like the river. You cannot swim against it so you must learn to swim with it. People need to upgrade themselves constantly. You have to consciously work to improve yourself. Let the creative juices flow. Let other vibrations other than your fixated ideas and egoistic stands come and flow through your home and environment. Don't be afraid. Read new authors. Learn a new trade. Take up some hobby like Painting, Photography or Music. Go away into another dimension for a while.

Such people are rarely sick, never depressed, get over hurts, view life as a possibility arena. Mentally they have tuned themselves to the idea of newness in their lives. They are ever young. They go through disappointments like everybody else but outgrow it as if overnight. There is always another sunset to go out and see. Not only imbibe this spirit but give this gift to your children.

44) Dr PK's Holistic Medico Advisory shared Dr. Detox'sphoto.

When we raise our voices to make a point, we are literally using physical means to ram down our words into the block-head in front of us.
This is extremely bad for your health as well as your relationship. The symptoms one generates are very similar to those of a stroke.
And deaths due to strokes are not unknown from anger bursts. Mild, regular anger bursts can easily becomes habits with autocratic people and I have known many people who eventually ended up with paralysis in their final days.
Marriage is a good cure. The need to adjust is a form of yoga that perforce makes you consider your own responses, restrain yourself, teach yourself selflessness and patience and caring for others. Quarrels that happen will teach you how helpless and vulnerable you are and force you to reorganise yourself and your persona. It is a sweet trap to make your obstacle-full life bearable as the final goal of The Creator is to help you grow into a more Divine you.

10% of conflicts is due to difference in opinion and 90% is due to wrong tone of voice.

rawforbeauty.com

45) <u>Dr PK's Holistic Medico Advisory</u> shared <u>Caregiver Resource Inc</u>'s <u>photo</u>.

My greatest standby, fast food and perfect meal has always been a Banana Sandwich. I survived traveling as a vegetarian in Europe on this. Slices of banana between 2 slices of whole wheat raisin bread, with yogurt if available or pineapple slices or even some soft cheese or mango on the side.
Something as simple as eating a few bananas can help keep you feeling positive and good inside...
When we travel, we keep bananas always with us in the sundry basket. It is the most wonderfully packaged fast food that you can think of that will keep you going till the next stop.

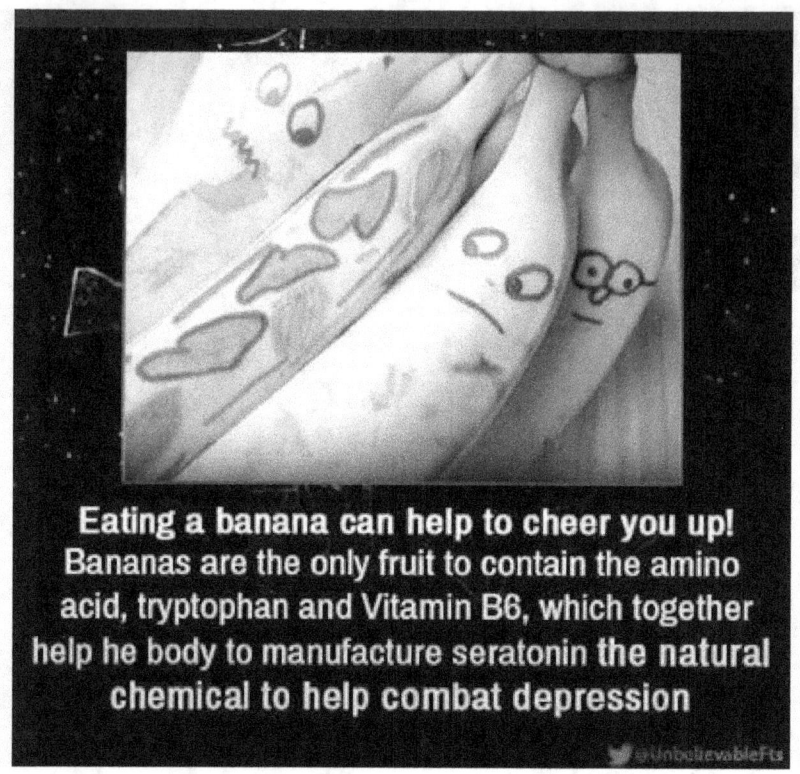

Eating a banana can help to cheer you up!
Bananas are the only fruit to contain the amino acid, tryptophan and Vitamin B6, which together help he body to manufacture seratonin **the natural chemical to help combat depression**

46) Eating Methodology.

Eat dessert first.

I practice it. Rajasthani families all follow this method of eating. Even my doctor uncle use to advise to eat sweets first, so that once the gastric juices are strongly established in the stomach, food is not only well digested, the chances of an infection are become negligible.

It seems rather logical to want to eat sugar first as the sugar levels are low when hungry and that is the time when I relish dessert most. Once the tummy is full, all desire to eat evaporates – unless one is in the habit of overeating as a matter of course.

THE AYURVEDIC WAY (

Ancient wisdom suggests if you start your meal with heavy and sweet food, then move on to the savoury part, and finally finish off with salad, you'll digest better and also manage to keep the flab away

Supriya Sharma

Ayurvedic cooking is about foods that suit your *dosha* (constitution). It involves a balanced meal, which nourishes and fulfills the requirements of the body, builds immunity, heals the body, aids digestion and eliminates waste. To avoid contracting season-specific illnesses, ayurveda recommends seasonal diets to help the body acclimatise to the season; warm spices and heavy grains on cold winter days and lighter foods such as fruits and vegetable salads during summer.

How to get started
To start with an ayurvedic way of life, have a good look at your current diet and try consuming foods with fewer preservatives, artificial colours and chemicals. Check out how much of frozen, fried and fermented foods form your diet and find out if you can replace them with freshly-cooked meals.

Identify your *dosha* (*vata, pitta, kapha*) based on your physical attributes and emotional strength. *Doshas* define the requirements of your body and lifestyle. If you have a thin, long frame, are lively, chatty and always on the move, you have a *vata* constitution. Try to include warm, moist ingredients like ghee, oils, ginger, garlic and eggs in your meals. People with a *pitta dosha* are intense, intelligent, and goal-oriented and have a vi-

> TO ACHIEVE GOOD HEALTH, IT'S ESSENTIAL TO DIGEST THE MEAL AND ASSIMILATE THE NUTRIENTS WELL; MEALTIME PLAYS AN IMPORTANT ROLE

47)   Dr PK shared <u>Kelly the Kitchen Kop</u>'s <u>photo</u>.

Yes I use this knowledge with good effect. Refelxology & Shiatsu is safe and emotionally soothing. The child feels comforted and cuddles to sleep.

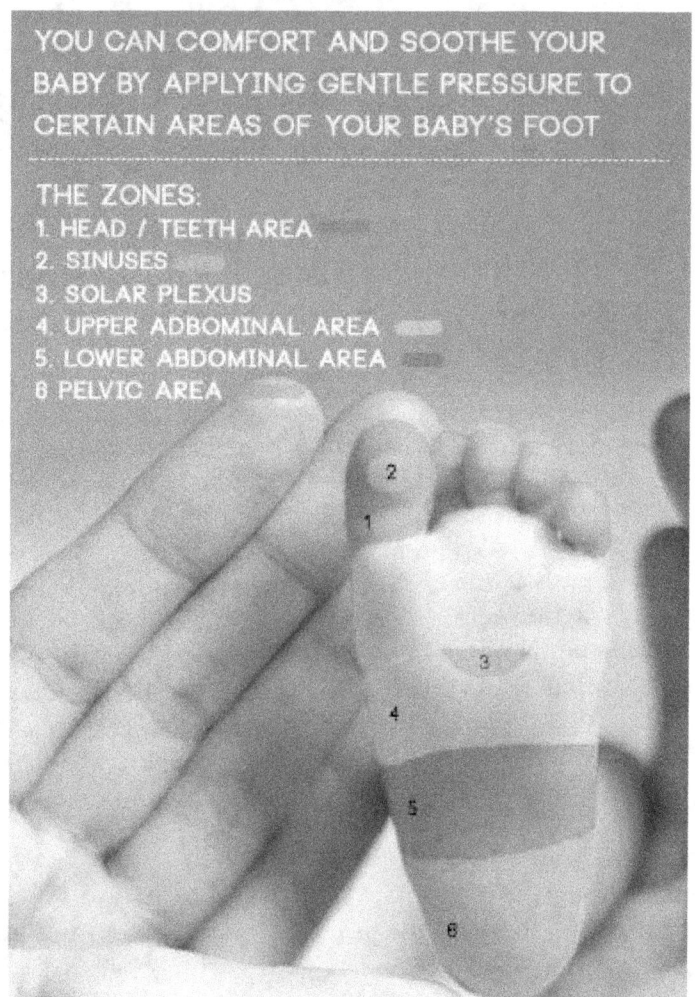

YOU CAN COMFORT AND SOOTHE YOUR
BABY BY APPLYING GENTLE PRESSURE TO
CERTAIN AREAS OF YOUR BABY'S FOOT

THE ZONES:
1. HEAD / TEETH AREA
2. SINUSES
3. SOLAR PLEXUS
4. UPPER ADBOMINAL AREA
5. LOWER ABDOMINAL AREA
6 PELVIC AREA

48) <u>Dr PK's Holistic Medico Advisory</u> shared<u>PsychopathFree</u>'s <u>photo</u>.

Interiorisation of nervous energies.

I bring up this subject because this is part of our reality. Otherwise lovely people who are actually sick, weak or deformed in their persona - they engender so much discord, negative emotions around them that it is time we gave it full credence for what it is and see how they create sickness by first giving birth to depression and through it to other manifestations

GASLIGHTING

A favorite tactic of manipulators, used to obstruct and distort their victim's understanding of reality. Intentionally setting up misdeeds, and then questioning the victim's sanity for reacting to those misdeeds. Rewriting history, or blatantly denying that the event ever took place. First, provoking negative emotions, then dismissing the victim's legitimate concerns with labels like "crazy", "insane", "bipolar", "hysterical", and "sensitive". Gaslighters are patronizing, unapologetic, and above all, they are cowardly. Because they are unable to manipulate healthy individuals, they must first manufacture insanity and chaos. This gives them the power & control that they seek over loving, compassionate human beings.

Learn the signs. Find your freedom.
RedFlags.PsychopathFree.com

of real sickness due to the interiorisation of nervous energies of the negative kind - we have this expression "broken heart" it is true. The illnesses that normally occur are centered around the heart, colon besides the psycho-effects.

Because they are unable to manipulate healthy individuals, psychopaths must first manufacture insanity and chaos. This gives them the power & control that they seek over loving, compassionate human beings.

49) Essential blood tests.

In today's technological life-style where illness and stresses re masked by drugs, illnesses fester in the body without we being aware of it. Warning tests, simple blood tests, should be taken as and when we feel something is not quite right. Of these I feel the three main tests are ESR,

Haemoglobin count (even a routine blood picture to be on the safe side) and this CEA test.

If you see the report below, normal is 0-3 and cancers are in the region of 40-70. This is a huge gap. People go on merrily until definitely they are diagnosed with cancer. It is astonishing that this can happen. One has to be totally unaware or blind or overconfidently suppressing all signals from the body. This can be nothing but supreme stupidity.

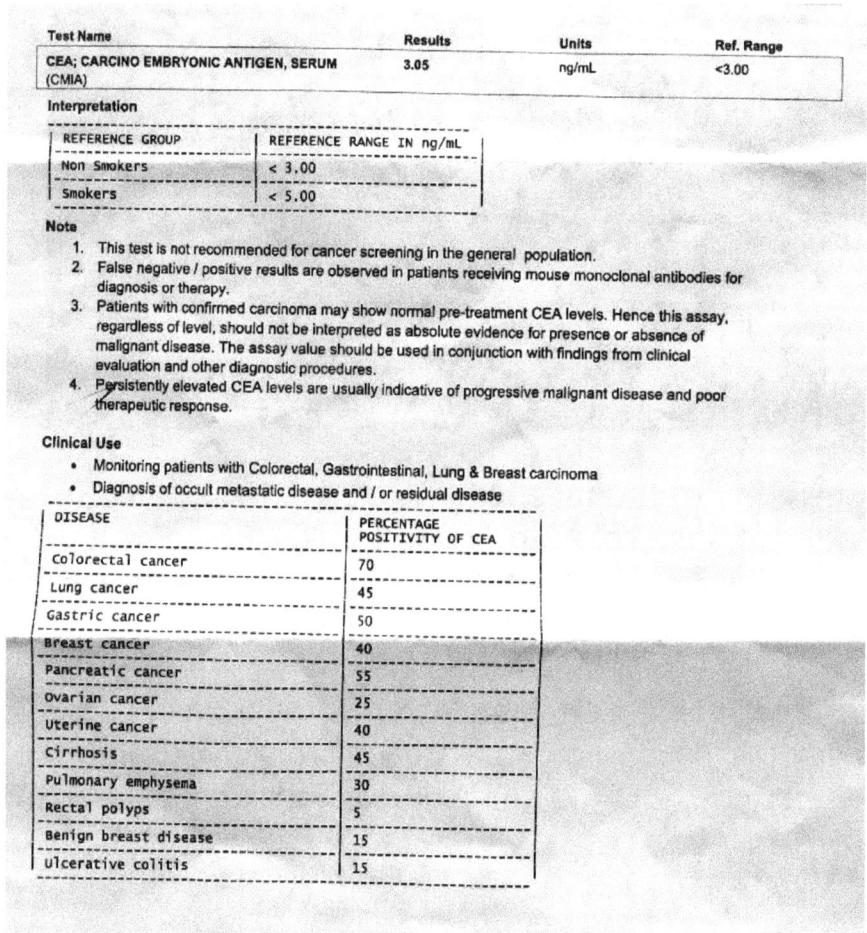

Test Name	Results	Units	Ref. Range
CEA; CARCINO EMBRYONIC ANTIGEN, SERUM (CMIA)	3.05	ng/mL	<3.00

Interpretation

REFERENCE GROUP	REFERENCE RANGE IN ng/mL
Non Smokers	< 3.00
Smokers	< 5.00

Note

1. This test is not recommended for cancer screening in the general population.
2. False negative / positive results are observed in patients receiving mouse monoclonal antibodies for diagnosis or therapy.
3. Patients with confirmed carcinoma may show normal pre-treatment CEA levels. Hence this assay, regardless of level, should not be interpreted as absolute evidence for presence or absence of malignant disease. The assay value should be used in conjunction with findings from clinical evaluation and other diagnostic procedures.
4. Persistently elevated CEA levels are usually indicative of progressive malignant disease and poor therapeutic response.

Clinical Use

- Monitoring patients with Colorectal, Gastrointestinal, Lung & Breast carcinoma
- Diagnosis of occult metastatic disease and / or residual disease

DISEASE	PERCENTAGE POSITIVITY OF CEA
Colorectal cancer	70
Lung cancer	45
Gastric cancer	50
Breast cancer	40
Pancreatic cancer	55
Ovarian cancer	25
Uterine cancer	40
Cirrhosis	45
Pulmonary emphysema	30
Rectal polyps	5
Benign breast disease	15
Ulcerative colitis	15

More on the CEA blood test.
It is really surprising that every 3rd person one meets today is talking of cancer in their household/family. How dormant have our senses become? Or is it the mistake of the medical professionals who keep treating the symptoms and miss the basic illness that is slowly birthing within? I would

say both. Our responsibility to ourselves is greater and we need to become more aware to the changing world, the effects of technological changes around us in our environment and foods and living styles that we are adopting – which are not always good for our health.

Any way the point is that this CEA test is a great pointer.

I would recommend that if you live in polluted cities and areas, you take this test on your own every now and then after the age of 40. Notice the chart. They show 0-3 as normal and the nearest danger signal is already at five. So 3 is already borderline dangerous.

If you detect higher scores you should immediately changes your life style eating habits by incorporating the following and allow your body to regain its natural balance:

More walks in the morning sunshine.
Eat foods that make your ph level alkaline.
Adopt cooking that leaves nutritive properties of the foods intact, use the most health giving ingredients and stop going for taste but aim for goodness.
Sleep and eat with the sun's circadian rhythm.
Mentally stop trying to worry too much about the world, others around you and managing it.

50) Dr PK's Holistic Medico Advisory shared Allen Hanes'sphoto.

WE collect illnesses like we do "concepts, thoughts, rules and prejudices". The mind is like a box. Soon we fill it up and call all the goodies "My Posessions". We become inordinately proud of all the valuables we have there-in. So much so that we refuse to entertain an exchange or change. From this comes the French expression "idée-fixe". The box gets totally crammed-up. This is the point when we stop learning but vehemently, more and more, wherever and however far our influence is accepted, we IMPOSE ourselves – quite mercilessly.

Love sometimes wants to do us a great favor: hold us upside down and shake all the nonsense out.

Hafiz

Making life difficult for everyone and involuntarily ours own. It is sickness causing and strokes are common in this kind of atmosphere.
Why is it so important to be "Never Wrong"?..... and to prove the others "Always in error"?

51) <u>Dr PK's Holistic Medico Advisory</u> shared <u>Awaken'sphoto</u>.

How we spread illness...
1) by ignoring the signals of the body like aches and pains + emotional discomfort
2) worse - ignoring symptoms of sickness like simple sore throats, ulcers in the mouth, constipation, restless legs, low back pain.
3) even worse - we pass on the stress to children whose concerns we ignore or try to cover up with food (mostly tasty comfort foods that is junk in nutrients) or expensive toys and things.

Stress

is an alarm clock that let's you know you are attached to something that's not true for you
-- Byron Katie

www.breakingfreefromlimits.com

52) Dr PK's Holistic Medico Advisory

Drug companies learnt from Mother Nature and then created new products that are easy to administer and use. So convenient that we forgot the natural products that not only give us relief but also give us the necessary nutrients and strengthen our metabolism. Here are 4 of them.

HOW DOES SESAME SEED OIL LOWER BLOOD PRESSURE?

SESAME IS THOUGHT to ORIGINATE in the INDUS VALLEY. IT IS One of the FIRST CROPS to BE PROCESSED for OIL.

SESAME SEED OIL CONTAINS THE POTENT ANTIOXIDANTS SESAMIN, SESAMOL AND OTHER LIGNANS, AS WELL AS VITAMIN E, CALCIUM, IRON AND MAGNESIUM. AFTER 60 DAYS, HYPERTENSIVE STUDY PARTICIPANTS' BLOOD PRESSURE HAD RETURNED TO WITHIN THE NORMAL RANGE.

DO PRUNES REALLY WORK FOR TREATING CONSTIPATION?

A NEW STUDY HAS REVEALED THAT, GIVEN THEIR PALATABILITY, TOLERABILITY, AVAILABILITY AND EFFICACY, DRIED PLUMS (PRUNES) SHOULD BE CONSIDERED A FIRST LINE OF DEFENSE IN TREATING MILD TO MODERATE CONSTIPATION.

IS THERE A NATURAL REMEDY FOR DEPRESSION?

SAFFRON IS native to GREECE and SOUTHEAST ASIA. IT WAS FIRST CULTIVATED in GREECE.

IN A SIX-WEEK HEAD-TO-HEAD STUDY PITTING PROZAC AGAINST THE SPICE SAFFRON, THOSE WHO TOOK SAFFRON CAPSULES FOUND THE SAFFRON TO BE EQUAL TO PROZAC AT RELIEVING SYMPTOMS OF DEPRESSION. THE SAFFRON, HOWEVER, DIDN'T PRODUCE SIDE EFFECTS.

WHAT'S GOOD ABOUT HEMP SEEDS?

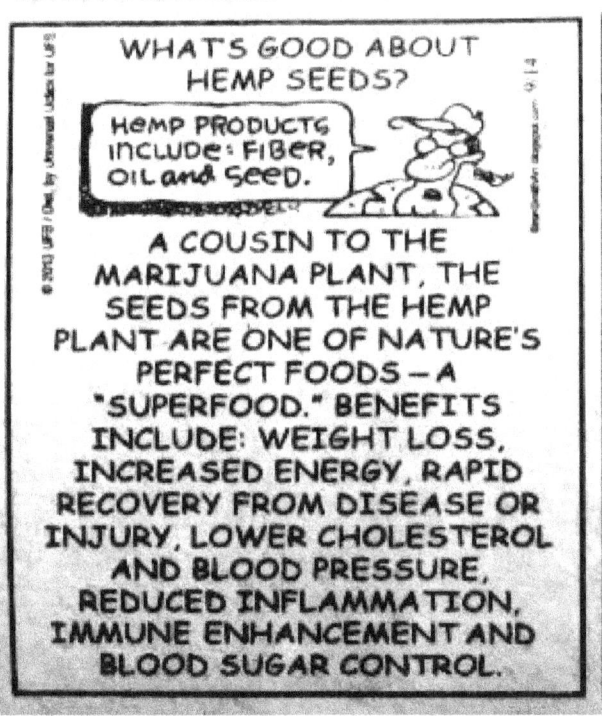

HEMP PRODUCTS INCLUDE: FIBER, OIL and SEED.

A COUSIN TO THE MARIJUANA PLANT, THE SEEDS FROM THE HEMP PLANT ARE ONE OF NATURE'S PERFECT FOODS — A "SUPERFOOD." BENEFITS INCLUDE: WEIGHT LOSS, INCREASED ENERGY, RAPID RECOVERY FROM DISEASE OR INJURY, LOWER CHOLESTEROL AND BLOOD PRESSURE, REDUCED INFLAMMATION, IMMUNE ENHANCEMENT AND BLOOD SUGAR CONTROL.

53) <u>Dr PK's Holistic Medico Advisory</u> shared <u>Ayurveda'sphoto</u>.

Onions have a cleansing action in the human body and raise immune levels but when they are fried with tomatoes to make Indian curry we are making a devilish base for highly difficult to digest curry which is responsible for much acid formation and big bellies to boot because the wonderful taste makes people over eat.
This is the base of Mughlai cooking which is easy on the tongue but makes the body sleepy & spiritless and prone to arterial blocks + sluggish colon. Everyone has heard of Tandoori chicken and Kashmiri Aloo(potato) dum or the Indian fast food item known as Chole(chickpeas) Bhatura(fried bread made from refined wheat dough).

1. Onions have anti-biotic, antiseptic, antimicrobial and carminative properties to help you stay away from infections.
2. Onions are rich in sulphur, fibers, potassium, vitamin B, vitamin C and they are low in fat, cholesterol and sodium.
3. It is an immediate cure for fever, common cold, cough, sore throat, allergies etc. A mixture of onion juice and honey can cure these problems easily.
4. A small piece of onion can work against side effects of fever if it's kept on the fore head.
5. A small piece of onion when inhaled can stop or slow down the bleeding through the nose.
6. An onion a day can cure insomnia or sleeping disorders. This will surely give you a good night sleep.
7. Onions can improve digestive system. If you have digestion problem, then onions can cure it by increasing the release of digestion juices.
8. Onion juice can cure burnt skin or an insect bite or a bee bite. It may burn more but it can heal it very effectively.
9. Onions can be used to prevent cancers. It works against head, neck and colon cancers.
10. You can protect yourself from Osteoporosis and Atherosclerosis by consuming onions daily.
11. Onions increases insulin in the body and also treats diabetes by controlling the sugar levels in the blood.

12. The bad cholesterol that causes heart problems can be burnt or removed if onions are consumed daily. It keeps you stay safe from the coronary diseases and also protects the good cholesterol.

13. Inflammation from Arthritis in the joints which can be healed with onions.

14. There is a small trick with onions to get some relief from body pains. Onions should be fried in sesame or castor oil and can be used to heal any aches.

23 Health Benefits Of Onions

www.curejoy.com – Expert Advice on Alternative Cure, Fitness & Beauty

15. One of the well-known tricks to remove dark patches or pigments on your face is to apply onion and turmeric juice on that area.

16. Onion juice is also used to cure ear and eye problems. This juice is used for infants as eye drops for clear vision.

17. This is also used for toothaches and tooth decaying.

18. Onions have rejuvenation properties on the body tissues.

19. For few types of moles, onion juice works efficiently by removing them.

20. For good memory and strong nervous system, consuming onions is your best bet.

21. Onions cure menstrual disorders. Raw onions should be consumed before a few days at the beginning of your cycle.

22. Use onion juice on the hair or the scalp to get rid of lice and hair fall. This is one of the most prominent of onion benefits for hair.

23. Onions contain water, protein, fats, starch, fibers, minerals, calcium, vitamin C, iron and B complex.

54) <u>Dr PK's Holistic Medico Advisory</u> shared <u>Gro Viste'sphoto</u>.

Why would anyone want to go to all the trouble of cooking when good nutritious food that collaborates with your body to prevent illness and keep one in top form is available ready-made. A beautiful fruit salad like this one with a dollop of ice cream is my idea of a feast.

I have been to many weddings where the spread is more than extensive. I gorge on the fruits, specially pineapple, mango, grapes, melons, guavas plums and such. Then, if available I take a light side dish of Chinese vegetable rice.

Every color has some vitamins peculiar to it. So eat fruits of all colors in plenty.

In today's world, this has become an acquired taste. It's a topsy-turvy world. I would say this should be our primary love while coffee would be the acquired taste.

55) Dr PK's Holistic Medico Advisory

The Sea as a valuable friend in sanity and physical well being.

The murmur of the waves is a highly tuned sound that lulls our agitated mind to rest. The constant movement of the waves with a breeze around us has a way to mesmerise us through the eyes and the breeze gives us an euphoric feeling. The vastness of the view stretches the spirit's aspiration to conceive big. All in all it has an expanding effect and even the cells of the body respond by joy.

In childhood, when we had a cut or two from our daily frolicking, and there were always 4-5 spots on our limbs that needed attention, our cure was a dip in the sea. It would cleanse away the wounds. I am aghast today to see the attention a minor abrasion gets.

I can't believe that tetanus shots are given as routine. It is criminal.

Here I am with my daughter, releasing my negativity in to the sea whose capacity to absorb is limitless + absorbing all its mighty strength of spirit. (in Pondicherry)

Note that the sea can absorb a lot of hurtful vibes and also give out a lot

of positivity. The phenomenon of weather where the sea absorbs the heat of the day and then dishes out a breeze at night is just the physical emanation of its spiritual activity.

Half of sicknesses come from the repressed irritations that continue to fester within, bringing the cells to boil like it happens in a microwave. The science of meditation is a good anti-dote. So is music and painting or playing a sport like table tennis and badminton which demands concentration elsewhere and gives the body a little to regroup its forces. Why are we in such a hurry to prejudge? Why do we feel superior enough to be judgmental with so much righteousness? The other day I was back in my old school which is an Ashram where the morning hours are for meditation and no other activity is encouraged especially in the meditation area and near it. I was sitting there; it was six in the morning. Just then an old lady comes, sees the latest newspaper daily

80

around nearby, left by another ashramite and asks me to tell her the cricket score. So I pick up the paper and open it. After all if the old lady is more interested in cricket scores and meditation is not her forte, who am I to judge? But before I could do my good karma, an old teacher of mine passes by and immediately scolds me for reading the paper in the meditation area! Boy, I was so amused. It was so much like my childhood when I was being scolded for something or the other, never heard nor given a chance to explain. I left immediately and went to the sea beach nearby to cleanse myself of the indignation that this teacher had injected in my atmosphere.

56) Dr PK's Holistic Medico Advisory shared Tantra'sphoto.

Show it with cuddles

Ah grapes.
When in college in Hyderabad, grape cultivation came to that area. In the beginning as it was a new product for that area, the market was limited and so the prices were low. It quickly became the poor man's food. And we gorged on it.

Grapes and raisins - I'll eat anything if accompanied by them.

Health Benefits of Grapes

The health benefits of grapes include its ability to treat constipation, indigestion, fatigue, kidney disorders, macular degeneration and prevention of cataract. Grapes, one of the most delicious fruits, are rich sources of vitamins A, C, B6 and folate in addition to essential minerals like potassium, calcium, iron, phosphorus, magnesium and selenium. Grapes contain flavonoids that are very powerful antioxidants, which can reduce the damage caused by free radicals and slacken ageing.

Grapes, owing to their high nutrient content, play an important role in ensuring a healthy and robust life.

Benefits: Some of the health benefits of grapes include the following:

Asthma: Due to its eminent therapeutic value, grapes can be used for cure of asthma. In addition to it, the assimilatory power of grapes is also higher. It increases the moisture present in lungs.

Heart diseases: Grapes increase the nitric oxide levels in the blood, which prevents blood clots thereby reducing the chances of heart attacks. In addition the antioxidant present in grapes prevents the oxidation of LDL cholesterol, which blocks the blood vessels.

Migraine: Ripe grape juice is an important home remedy for curing migraine. It should be taken early in the morning, without mixing additional water.

Constipation: Grapes are very effective in overcoming constipation. They are considered as a laxative food, as they contain organic acid, sugar and cellulose. They also relieve chronic constipation by toning up intestine and stomach.

Indigestion: Grapes play an important role in dyspepsia. They relieve heat and cure indigestion and irritation of the stomach. They are also preferred as they constitute a light food.

Fatigue: Light and white grape juice replenishes the iron content present in the body and prevents fatigue. Though, the dark grape juice might not give an iron boost and on the other hand, decrease the iron levels. Drinking grape juice also provides you with instant energy. The anti-oxidants present in grapes also provide the needed boost to your immune system.

Kidney disorders: Grapes can substantially reduce the acidity of the uric acid and helps in the elimination of the acid from the system, thereby reducing the work pressure of kidneys.

Breast cancer: Through a latest study, it has been discovered that purple colored Concord grape juice helps in preventing breast cancer. Significant reduction in mammary tumor mass of laboratory rats was seen after they were fed the grape juice on the experimental basis.

Alzheimer's disease: Resveratrol, a beneficial polyphenol present in grapes reduces the levels of amyloidal-beta peptides in patients with Alzheimer's disease. Studies suggest that grapes can enhance brain health and stall the onset of neurodegenerative diseases.

Macular degeneration: Grapes can prevent the age related loss of vision or macular degeneration. Three servings of grapes a day can reduce the risks of macular degeneration by over 36 %.

Prevents cataract: Flavonoids present in grapes have antioxidants, which can reduce and fight the damage caused by free radicals such as cataract apart from cardiovascular diseases, cancer, and age related problems.

Blood cholesterol: Grapes contain a compound called pterostilbene, which has the capacity to bring down cholesterol level. Saponins present in grape skin can also prevent the absorption of cholesterol by binding with it.

Antibacterial activity: Red grapes have strong antibacterial and antiviral properties and can protect you from infections. They have a strong antiviral property against poliovirus and herpes simplex virus.

Anticancer properties: Grapes are found to have strong anti cancer properties due to the anti-inflammatory effect of Resveratrol present in grapes. It is particularly effective in colorectal cancer and breast cancer. Anthocyanins and proanthocyanidins present in grapes have properties of an anti-proliferate and can inhibit the growth of cancer causing agents. Grape juice not just prevents the risk of cancer but also suppresses the growth and propagation of cancer cells. The pigments contained in grapes enhance the overall immunity of the body.

Thus, grapes play a pivotal role in preventing innumerable health disorders and can be used as home based remedies for several ailments. Dried grapes, known as raisins, are extremely nutritious and help in many disorders including constipation, acidosis, anemia, fever, sexual weakness and help in gaining weight and eye care. Read more about benefits of raisins.

58) Dr PK's Holistic Medico Advisory

Slowdown!
Most of our sicknesses are caused by auto-intoxication. This is the result of bad eating habits and bad elimination and often coupled with even poorer assimilation.
The solution is refraining from solid foods and taking in only liquids. In India buttermilk is considered the best. The fresher the better.
When I feel that my system is getting overwhelmed, I go on a buttermilk fast with occasional coffee for 3-5 days. This gives the body the chance to clear all backlog.

Cultured buttermilk is probably the easiest and most fool proof fermented milk product to make - nothing more than the liquid left after the butter is churned. Buttermilk is low in fat. It's sometimes tolerated by people with lactose intolerance since some of the lactose is fermented by bacteria. The acidity of buttermilk also explains its long refrigerator shelf life. Slightly sour in taste. It is quite popular as a coolant in India and a variant called "lassi" made from yoghurt is sold commercially. I prefer mine with a little salt and powdered roasted Cummins. Buttermilk can be found in supermarkets, in the dairy section, and is known as cultured buttermilk, which is made by adding a bacterial culture to low-fat or nonfat milk. For more authentic and tasty, though, there is churned buttermilk, which is the liquid that remains after milk is churned into butter. Buttermilk is used in many recipes to give it a creamy taste or texture.

59) Dr PK's Holistic Medico Advisory shared a link.

Do away with the barriers.
The amount of barriers to healing is a long and sordid list, with a dirty food, water and air supply sitting at the top. Combine that with a poor relationship with the sun and the earth, and true healing becomes very difficult. However, if we can reignite our connection with the earth, we may find healing becomes a lot easier.

What is earthing?
Earthing, also known as grounding, is based on research showing that having a connection to the earth's electrical energy promotes physical well-being. This connection is made between the electrical frequencies of the human body and that of the earth, which can be achieved directly (e.g., barefoot in grass or on a beach) or by proxy through grounding technology.

60) Dr PK's Holistic Medico Advisory

Dehydration is now a common debility accompanied with salt deficiency.

From a case diary (taken from the internet):
I muscle tested her and found that underlying her BP of 240/140 and the crushing pain in the head, her body's water content was only 6% (normal

is 75%), salt content was zero, potassium was 96% deficient, and cardiac output (blood flow from the heart) was only 40% (normal is 100%). So the blood supply to the head was 60% deficient.
Later....
she grew 2", because the salt and the water had refilled her compressed disc spaces in her vertebral column. The disc spaces had become compressed because they had become dehydrated since the fluid filling up these discs are 95% water.

Why salt? Because without salt the body cannot retain water no matter how much water is drunk. You will still be dehydrated because you will just keep urinating and sweating the water out.

On salt -
What is bad for hypertension is iodized salt, which is a fake salt. It is made up of only 3 synthetic chemicals, sodium, chloride, iodine. It takes long to dissolve in water (glistens like diamonds), does NOT dissolve in the body, does not get through the kidneys, gives kidney stones, and raises blood pressure.
The best salt is rock salt, has 72 natural minerals including natural sodium, chloride, iodine. It dissolves in water, absorbed in your body, does not produce kidney stones, and best of all brings down blood pressure and stops/prevents muscle cramps, numbness, tingling.

61) Dr PK's Holistic Medico Advisory

I do not wish to sound alarming but we surely should begin to ponder over the simple matter when we see that an estimated 600 million people worldwide today are suffering from increasing incidence of cancer, respiratory ailments, stress disorders, birth defects and reproductory problems both in the male and female. All of which can be traced to technological advances in every domain of our lives. Instead of using them in moderation to better our lives, we have let them overshadow and take-over our lives for the worse.

We brought the magnetic field effect into our homes with the TV and now the computer screens and heavy load products like the compressor in fridges and Air Conditioners. But enough is not enough. Then we went one step further with the microwave oven.

This much happiness was obviously not enough for the human race. So we developed the cell phone.
And then to make sure nothing was left to chance we are now going for wireless connectivity. This new trend towards wireless homes and offices is to my horror a step down to perdition. As individuals are we concerned? Is it not the industry's responsibility to take the righteous path and tell the public when a technology is not good for them and even go to the extent to refuse to promote it?

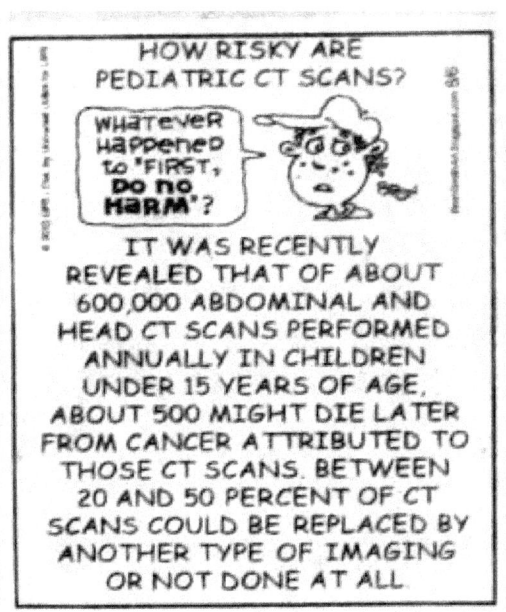

62) Dr PK's Holistic Medico Advisory shared Pradeep Pk Maheshwari's photo.

Read thru it. Bad!.
Reminds me of Thoreau's advice: simplify.
Humans are not ready for the windfall of plenty. They are hurting their selves.

You know the saying: Lord; don't give nails to the bald!
It is not about politics. It is about living. Our world is being damaged and possibly even destroyed by a modern demand to posses everything we can possibly imagine. This is real and it is happening now. It is an urgent burden that, I am convinced the earth and the life on it cannot bear. The pollution levels have reached seriously damaging levels.

63) <u>Dr PK's Holistic Medico Advisory</u> shared <u>Raising Ecstasy</u>'s <u>photo</u>.

In a way you can say, the heart simply gives up.
The spirit refuses to support living anymore.
The first cells to respond are the gut's negative flora. This creates situations which in their worst scenario can give colon cancer.
Depression and heart failures are common in this state.

Don't criticise others and don't let yourself be criticised. Run if possible from abusive people or learn to control the moment with calm and assured, logical behavior; thereby blunting the attack; still when it happens too often, it will hurt and damage surely.

You certainly have better thing to do than "manage" with nasty people who use constructive criticism as an excuse to boost their own egos.

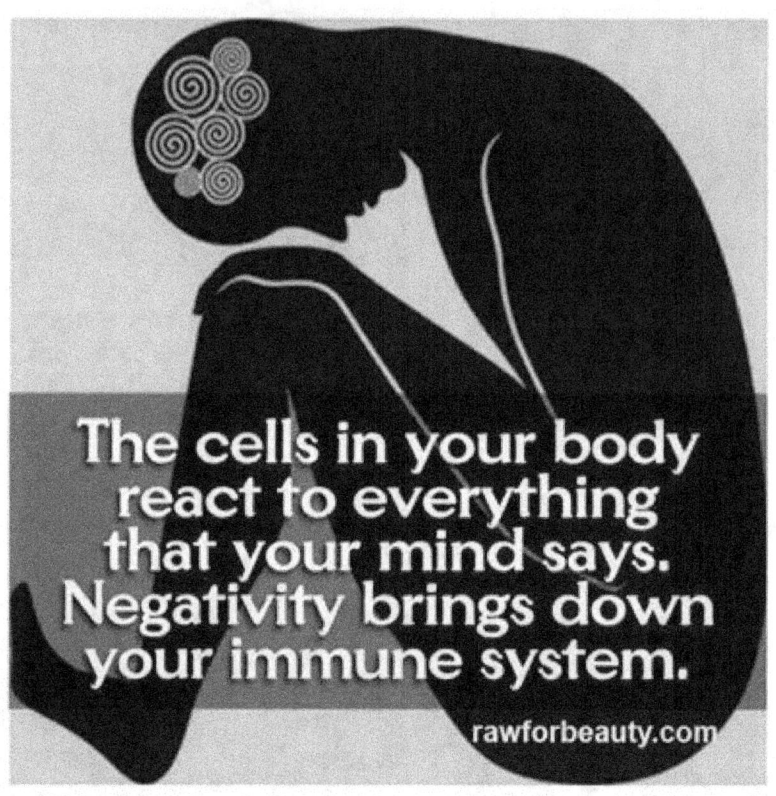

The cells in your body react to everything that your mind says. Negativity brings down your immune system.

rawforbeauty.com

64) Dr PK's Holistic Medico Advisory

12 Foods Most People Don't Know Are Dyed or Adulterated
January 16, 2014 | By Karen Foster/WakingTimes

1. ORANGE CHEDDAR

To my knowledge there are no cows that produce orange milk. Yet, a majority of consumers are unaware that orange cheddar is dyed. Cheddar cheese acquired its classic orange color from annatto in the 1800's when it was thought that high quality cheeses were yellow due to higher quality green grass fed to cattle. Annatto is known as the "poor man's saffron" because it can be used to achieve a similar bright yellow color to saffron without the high price. Natural annatto is not itself toxic to human health, however there are some processed forms of annatto which are completely synthetic. This is often not clearly labeled on cheddar cheese ingredient lists and synthetic forms are often being labeled as "color added" rather than "artificial color". This creates an allergenic potential and endangers consumer safety while providing difficult challenges for consumers who experience reactions since they may relate allergic reactions to intolerance of cheese rather than the color, although both may occur. Annatto is also added to butter, ghee and margarine.

Solution: Stick to white cheddar. All cheese should be white or slightly off white.

2. OLIVE OIL

Olive oil is one of the most adulterated foods on Earth. The worst part is that there is little regulation or oversight on what constitutes virgin olive oils. To boost profits, for example, some producers have been caught adulterating the oil they label as "extra virgin" with much cheaper hazelnut, soy, or sunflower seed oil, among others, as well as mislabeling its country of origin. And they keep doing it because the profits in adulterating olive oil are "comparable to cocaine trafficking, with none of the risks." Often the well-known brand-name olive oil companies you're familiar with may not even realize that this trick has been pulled on them by unscrupulous suppliers halfway around the world-but you wind up with adulterated oil in your kitchen and on your food just the same. In recent years olive oil was the most adulterated agricultural product in the European Union, prompting the E.U.'s anti-fraud office to establish an olive-oil task force.

Solution: Unless you have a very good nose, you may not be able to tell the difference if an olive oil has been adulterated or not. Don't worry about colour. Good oils come in all shades, from green to gold to pale straw – but avoid flavours such as moldy, cooked, greasy, meaty, metallic, and cardboard. Ensure that your oil is labelled "extra virgin," since other categories-"pure" or "light" oil, "olive oil" and "olive pomace oil" – have undergone chemical refinement. If you are purchasing a full bottle of virgin olive oil for less than $10-$15 per bottle, there is a good chance it is adulterated. Since most extra virgin oil nowadays is made with centrifuges, it isn't "pressed" at all, and true extra virgin oil comes exclusively from the first processing of the olive paste. The absolute best olive oil is Ice-Pressed, a truly raw superfood.

3. TURMERIC POWDER

Turmeric powder is added to many foods to enhance yellow tints and colors. Although some ingredient lists will state turmeric, Metanil Yellow and Kesari Dal are often being added instead of turmeric. These adulterants are highly carcinogenic and if consumed over a continuous period of time it can also cause stomach disorders. Lead chromate powder has also been found in adulterated turmeric. Even raw turmeric powder sold as either pre-packaged or bulk has been found to be adulterated with these substitutes.

Solution:
If you purchased turmeric powder and suspect it may be adulterated, dissolve half a spoon full of the powder in 20 ml of lukewarm water. Add a few drops of lemon juice or any commonly available acid at home. If the water turns pink, violet or purple, it shows the presence of Metanil yellow.

4. BLACK PEPPER

Some manufacturers of black pepper are known to use papaya seeds to add bulk to their product. Papaya seeds in any modest quantity can cause serious liver problems and stomach disorders.

Solution:
Float the sample in alcohol. Mature black pepper corns will sink whereas papaya seeds will float to the surface.

5. WASABI

Most wasabi served at sushi restaurants is not real wasabi at all. It's usually made from horseradish powder mixed with green food coloring and dry mustard. Real wasabi is one of the rarest and most difficult

vegetables in the world to grow, which is why that fake stuff was created. The real thing is green Japanese horseradish root that gets mashed into paste and is incredibly spicy, and quite expensive.
Solution:
If you really want to know if the wasabi you are consuming is the real thing, the first clue is the color which is usually slightly paler than the fake stuff. Smell wise, the real rhizome will assault your nostrils with one whiff, causing the eyes to water instantly. Taste also goes to the real rhizome — the sushi bar stuff has a bit more 'heat' but the real stuff definitely has much more flavor.

6. PICKLED GINGER

Most of the processed pickled ginger (pink or golden yellow) that restaurants use is packed with aspartame and potassium sorbate, and some processors even use MSG. Aspartame, the main ingredient in Equal, NutraSweet and Spoonful, is an artificial sweetener. Potassium sorbate gets used as a preservative. Both are toxic. The pink ginger is dyed with red food coloring.

Solution:
Some attentive sushi chefs shave their own ginger and pickle it themselves, but you would need to inquire to find out.

7. CARMINIC ACID OR CARMINE

Another very popular method of introducing red and pink into foods is cochineal extract. Cochineal dye has been around for centuries, but most people are not aware it's crushed insect body parts. Sometimes it appears as carminic acid or carmine. The cochineal insect is native to Mexico and South America, and contrary to the popular nomenclature, they're not technically beetles.

Solution:
If this really grosses you out, read your ingredient lists and hopefully carminic acid or carmine will be listed instead of "added color" which could be anything.

8. GREEN CHILLIES, GREEN PEAS, OTHER GREEN VEGGIES

Some frozen varieties of these foods still contain Malachite Green to accentuate the bright, glowing green colour of the vegetable. Scientists have found that exposure to malachite green may raise the risk of cancer, cause genetic mutations, and harm the human reproductive system. It has been used as a fungicide in some countries but was supposed to be banned internationally in the 1990s.
Solution:
Take a small portion of the sample and place it over a moistened white blotting paper. Coloured impressions on the blotting paper indicate the presence of Malachite green.

9. BRIGHT RED MEAT

Although not a chemical dye, most meat eaters may be unaware that more than 70% of all beef and chicken in the United States, Canada and other countries is being treated with poisonous carbon monoxide gas. It can make seriously decayed meat look fresh for weeks. The meat industry continues to allow this toxic gas injection into many of the meat products people consume on a daily basis.
Solution:
Don't buy your meat at conventional grocery retailers. The CO gas is just a small part of the problem. Hormones, antibiotics, vaccines and other chemicals injected into cattle contribute to far worse health issues. If you must eat red meat, ensure it is organic, coming from pasture-fed animals.

10. CHILI POWDER

Believe or not but some loose and bulk chili powder is still adulterated with red brick powder or sawdust, for bulk. That's right! At some point in your life you've likely eaten chili powder that had construction materials in it.
Solution:

Only purchase organic brands of chili powder which are marginally more expensive and grown without any toxic chemicals.

11. GOLDEN HONEY

Most golden honey you see at your local grocery is dead and far from the health promoting powerhouse of its raw unpasteurized counterpart. Processed honey is not honey at all and if you desire any kind of health benefits, you must stick to the real stuff. But some golden honey is even adulterated with corn syrup, rice sugar and even water.
Solution:
A cotton wick dipped in pure honey burns when ignited with a matchstick. Natural honey will light the match easily and the flame will burn off the honey. Fake honey will not light because of the moisture it contains.

12. INSTANT COFFEE

Tamarind seeds or chicory powder are very popular adulterants around the world and used to add bulk and color to instant coffee. These can cause diarrhea, stomach disorders, giddiness and severe joint pains.

Solution:
Gently sprinkle coffee on the surface of water in a glass. The coffee will float whereas chicory will start to sink within a few seconds. Also, the falling chicory powder will leave a trail of colour behind due to the large amounts of caramel it contains.

65) Dr PK's Holistic Medico Advisory

Help yourself
The brain needs time to assimilate and refresh itself. Therefore going to bed early is a sound investment in your health.
This will ensure you follow Mother Earth's circadian rhythm, wake up fresh.
Additionally your elimination process will get time to its part properly.

It is best to divide the 24 hours in proper 12 hour periods. Eat and be active from 7 to 7 in the day and rest, relax for the rest.
Think again about those late nights

to go to bed earlier

A recent study has challenged the theory that sleep strengthens brain connections, while revealing that it is important because it weakens the connections among brain cells to save energy, avoid cellular stress and maintain the ability of neurons to respond selectively to stimuli. The synaptic homeostasis hypothesis of sleep, or 'SHY', which takes into account years of evidence from human and animal studies, was recently conducted by leading sleep scientists, who said that while a person is awake, learning strengthens the synaptic connections throughout the brain, increasing the need for energy and saturating the brain with new information. Sleep allows the brain to reset, helping integrate newly learned material with consolidated memories, so the brain can begin anew the next day. Thus, sleep helps the brain renormalize strength based on a comprehensive sampling of its overall knowledge of the environment. **ANI**

66) <u>Dr PK's Holistic Medico Advisory</u> shared <u>Juicing For Health</u>'s <u>photo</u>.

I would like this:
HEALTHY KIDNEY SUPPORT

The diuretic properties of this juice combo effectively removes toxic wastes from the body through frequent urination. Thus, it helps to ...

- Prevent formation of kidney stones.
- Promote healthy kidneys.
- Naturally lower blood pressure.
- Eliminate uric acid that causes gout.
- Reduce inflammation that causes rheumatism and swelling.
- Rid the body of excess fluid (water retention).

JUICE RECIPE:
- 1 cucumber

- ½ fennel
- 4 ribs of celery
- 2 green apples
- ¼ lemon
- 1-inch ginger root (optional)

HEALTHY KIDNEY SUPPORT
By: Juicing-for-Health.com

JUICE RECIPE:
- 1 cucumber
- ½ fennel
- 4 ribs of celery
- 2 green apples
- ¼ lemon
- 1-inch ginger root

67) **Dr PK's Holistic Medico Advisory** shared Caregiver Resource Inc's photo.

When the liver goes, the rest of the body goes with it.
Reduce intake of contaminants and acidic foods.

Changing a few habits can make all the difference....

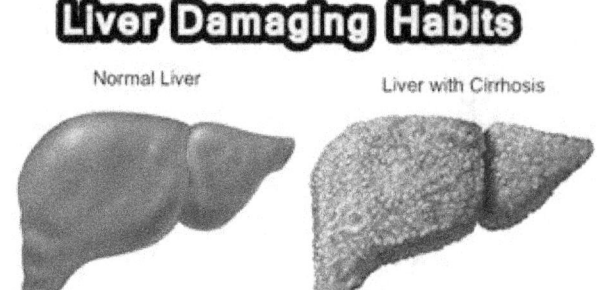

Liver Damaging Habits

Normal Liver   Liver with Cirrhosis

1. Sleeping too late and waking up too late are main cause.
2. Not urinating in the morning.
3. Too much eating.
4. Skipping breakfast.
5. Consuming too much medication.
6. Consuming too much preservatives, additives, food coloring, and artificial sweetener.   missclinic.com

68) Dr PK's Holistic Medico Advisory shared The Mystic's Quotes's photo.

Leave no place for depression in your life.
Depression is not just bad moods. It is a corrosive acid that hurts the body and dirties the mind, leaving a trail of toxic build-up behind it as it moves and permeates the rest of our being
Intense living...With focus and clearly thought out objective - from my vantage point, I would say this is the only way to savor life. The act of

trying to get started on this path itself is very interesting and enjoyable. Your time available doubles or trebles. Results are more often to our satisfaction and wishes - even if they aren't, we just have no time to mope.

69) <u>Dr PK's Holistic Medico Advisory</u> shared a <u>link</u>.
A good approach.

Mushrooms substituted for meat? This new weight management trick is proven to help cut calories!

foodtank.com

A recent study suggests using mushrooms in place of meat will help reduce one day's calorie count by 123 calories.

Shame on you Earthlings for bringing this pestilence on your own people. This is so heart breaking. The demineralization/denaturalisation of food is behind this tragedy.

Transfats "nice" looking, non-rancid going, "nice" looking, white & clean and soft bake flours, nice looking highly concentrated sugars + coloring, chemicals and preservatives.

Now everyone is fed they said! They made money from both the feeding and then from the treating.

HOW EARLY DOES HEART DISEASE START?

YOUR CHILD MAY aLReaDY the Have eaRLy SiGnS of HeaRT DiSease.

OF 300 KOREAN WAR SOLDIERS AUTOPSIED IN 1953, 77 PERCENT HAD "GROSS VISIBLE EVIDENCE" OF CORONARY ARTERY DISEASE. SOME HAD CORONARY ARTERIES THAT WERE 90 PERCENT BLOCKED. THEIR AVERAGE AGE: 22 YEARS OLD. FATTY STREAKS, THE FIRST EVIDENCE OF ATHEROSCLEROSIS, HAVE BEEN FOUND IN MORE THAN HALF OF ALL THE HEARTS OF AUTOPSIED CHILDREN BY AGE 10.

71)   For Diabetics.

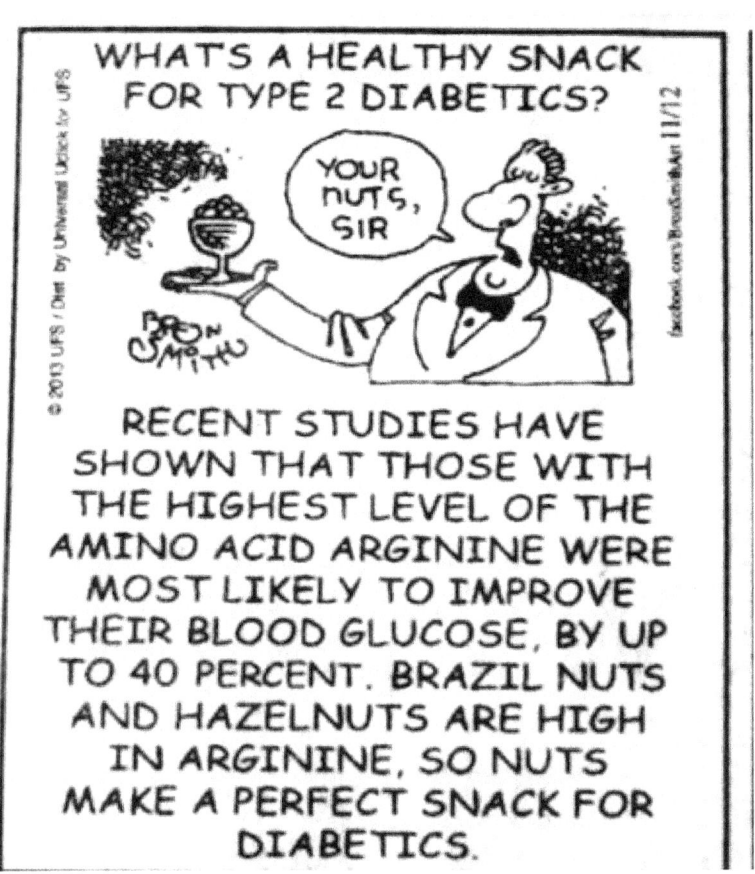

72) Dr PK's Holistic Medico Advisory

Many new processes and foods were introduced without fully understanding the final repercussions and their effects on the human system. The whole food chain has changed and so has the body's responses. Here are five foods that merit a little more understanding and perhaps not used at all.

By Derek Henry
The five organic foods to watch as they may be hurting you

Wheat

Wheat has enjoyed a long run of being the darling of the grains but in recent years has taken a serious hit, with gluten sensitivity plaguing people.

It's not that organic wheat is necessarily bad in and of itself, but rather, our digestive systems have become severely compromised, and as a result we lack the friendly bacteria that helps digest this component of wheat which leaves many people in pain and distress.

This may be partially alleviated for some by simply consuming wheat that is only sprouted, but for many, this will still not resolve the issue.

Wheat can be substituted in a number of ways, the more popular being amaranth, oats, almond, coconut, millet, buckwheat, corn, rice and quinoa flour.

Soy

Soy was at the tip of everyone's tongues when the soy industry convinced us that their products were not only safe for consumption but also actually good for you.

However, research is starting to uncover the opposite. Soy has now been attributed to endocrine disruption, digestive problems, hormone issues, thyroid challenges and fertility complications.

Soy promoters deny this research and point to epidemiological studies of Asians and their reduced rates of breast and prostate cancers, even though their traditional diet is soy-dominated. However, these studies fail to point out that these soy products are primarily fermented, which creates health-promoting probiotics that facilitate proper digestion.

Choose soy products that are organic and fermented.

Peanut butter

Peanuts, unlike hard-shelled nuts, are encased in a very soft and porous shell, which allows contaminants such as fungi to bind to them. As a result, aflatoxin, a cancer-causing chemical produced by naturally occurring fungi in the soil, can easily attach itself to the developing nut.

Since systematic fungal infections are affecting 70% of people, it may not be a wise idea to consume a food that naturally contains it, as it can exacerbate the problem and cause severe reactions and even death.

If you do choose to buy organic peanut butter, refrigerate it at all times to inhibit the growth of this naturally occurring fungus.

Cow's milk

Organic cow's milk eliminates some of the primary concerns of consuming milk, namely antibiotics, hormones and other chemicals.

However, organic milk is also commonly pasteurized which effectively removes all beneficial bacteria and enzymes and makes it much more difficult for the human digestive tract to properly break down and absorb it.

If you choose organic cow's milk, look for raw.

Pork

Pigs are dirty animals and eat everything in sight (including their own feces). Since their digestive systems work quickly, there is no opportunity to eliminate any toxins that may be present in what they eat.

Not only that, but a pig also does not have any sweat glands, which takes away an effective toxin removal process, allowing more toxins to stay inside their body.

Even though organically raised pigs should have toxin-free diets, there is great difficulty in monitoring and circumventing their insatiable desire to eat nearly everything in sight.

Instead of pork, try turkey bacon or organic, grass-fed beef, which is much friendlier to your intestinal system.

73) Dr PK's Holistic Medico Advisory

You don't have to be doing regular formal yoga. You can do freehand stretching exercises simply in your daily routine. It is a good practice to stretch well on waking up.

The stretching postures keep your muscles elongated, and prevents many of the structural problems of ageing...

74) Dr PK's Holistic Medico Advisory – Proteins for vegetarians

It's not like you'd ask a Gorilla where it gets its protein from, would you? As science continues to shed light on the health benefits associated with eating less meat and more 'earthly' foods like organic fruits and vegetables, more people around the globe are making a transition to a vegetarian and/or vegan diet for a variety of reasons. There is a reason why a plant based diet can help prevent over 60% of chronic disease deaths.

Research indicates that rates of heart disease and certain cancers are strongly associated with animal-protein based diets. Plant based foods on the other hand has plenty of protein and calcium along with far greater amounts of other essential nutrients like antioxidants and complex carbohydrates that you won't find in meat or dairy products.

This is happening in other countries too where modernisation and factory made foods have become welcome.

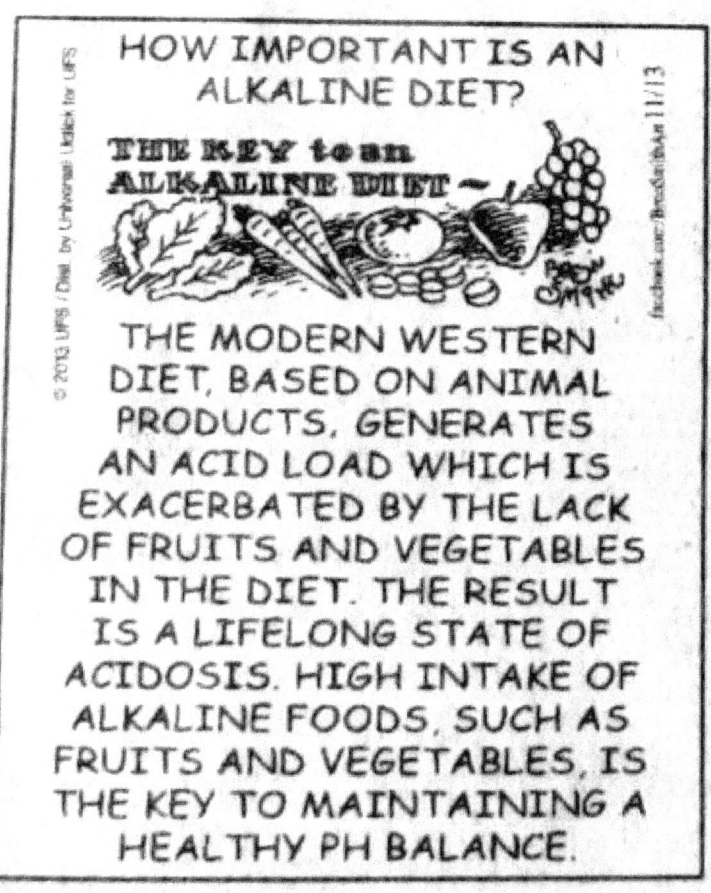

HOW IMPORTANT IS AN ALKALINE DIET?

THE KEY to an ALKALINE DIET ~

THE MODERN WESTERN DIET, BASED ON ANIMAL PRODUCTS, GENERATES AN ACID LOAD WHICH IS EXACERBATED BY THE LACK OF FRUITS AND VEGETABLES IN THE DIET. THE RESULT IS A LIFELONG STATE OF ACIDOSIS. HIGH INTAKE OF ALKALINE FOODS, SUCH AS FRUITS AND VEGETABLES, IS THE KEY TO MAINTAINING A HEALTHY PH BALANCE.

75) <u>Dr PK's Holistic Medico Advisory</u>

CONJUNCTIVITIS

Conjunctivitis has good reasons to be considered a little dangerous. One, it is easily transmitted and it affects the eyes that make you incapable of work or anything else.

Eyes are particularly sensitive to attack, as they are open to airborne allergens. In today's polluted world the situation has only gotten worse. Unknowingly we tend to rub or clean our eyes with dirty hands now and then. It is a miracle that we don't have a reaction all the time.

The best medicine, of course, is prevention, which is as is obvious to the most cursory glance, perfect in theory but impossible in practice. Every bill of exchange, every file we touch, every door-knob or tap in the toilet has had the impression of many hands and the hygiene of these hands would be impossible to trace and even if known, difficult to prevent from making an inroads into our own hands.

Frequent washing of the hands is a good idea in the circumstances.

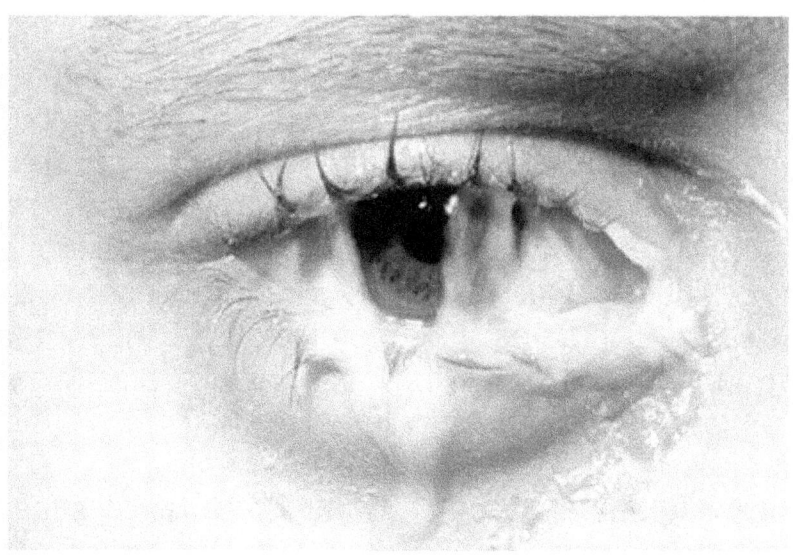

76) <u>Dr PK's Holistic Medico Advisory</u>

HAIR AND DIET

Hair is mostly a kind of protein.
The hair, like every other part of us, depends on good nutrition and good circulation to stay healthy. It is a vital indicator of our general health and chemical analysis of hair is as potent an indicator as blood tests. A vitamin A deficiency results in dry, lifeless hair and often dandruff. The protein Keratin is the main component of hair; therefore a shortage of protein can result in hair loss. Specially in vegetarians or food faddists who do not eat balanced diets. B vitamins are extremely important. These water-based vitamins tend to be generally deficient because they are easily washed out of the system. The fault may be in the cooking methodology or intake of drinks like tea, coffee or colas. The B vitamins that are especially associated with hair color are folic acid, choline, pantothenic acid, paraaminobenzoic acid and biotin. A deficiency of copper can also result in premature graying. Hair loss is often associated with lack of amino acids and B vitamins. The minerals calcium, copper and iron are needed for strong healthy strands.

Since vitamins and minerals are interdependent and work together, they are most effective when taken as part of a good diet. For instance, the vitamins mentioned above will need vitamin E, C, the entire range of B and zinc in particular to be absorbed and utilised by the body. For a lustrous mane, therefore eat whole grains, wheat germ, brewer's yeast, liver if you are a meat eater, plenty of fresh green salads, raw and short cooked vegetables like the Chinese do, and fresh fruits properly washed to remove any residues of pesticides. As a general recommendation, we can advise the use of Schussler's Biochemic salts, which are available in all homoeopathic medicine shops. If possible include seaweed formulations in your diet, such as spirulina.

Your hair is throwing out matured cells all the time. This may be dandruff or mistaken as dandruff but it may also be dried shampoo. So make sure.

The life we are leading today is murder to hair. Antibiotics, pollution in the air and water, smoking and exhausts from cars are playing havoc. To vegetarians I would suggest yoghurt made from unprocessed milk and to non-vegs I would advise lean meats.

May you have beautiful hair for the rest of your life!

77) Dr PK's Holistic Medico Advisory

Why are we so bent on killing ourselves?

You might as well suffocate yourself with a plastic bag over your head - considering the environment we have created and the life we are leading.

Let's see where we are going wrong in general. How the body is becoming weak and its natural self-curing mechanism is not working. Let's begin with normal drinking habits. Colas, coffees, teas, and alcohol have overtaken the processing capacity of the body, draining & leeching out precious vitamins and minerals, which are not being replaced. At the same time bladders are under pressure and the quality of urine is terribly concentrated which in turn irritates the bladder. Whatever happened to clean old water and juices?

In our hurry to get things done to earn more money to gather more comforts we have lost out on natural foods and we are consuming denatured food and moving about less too. The digestion is incomplete and the assimilation is even less efficient.

This results in GERD conditions & constipation. Constipation in turn results in auto-intoxication. This is the mother of all diseases. When the toxins won't go out, they will get stored and edge out the good guys and quietly infect every cell and pore of the body.

The very first symptoms can be skin allergies or sniffles and colds. Go in for a detox program on your own. This is simple. Avoid cereals. Drink fluids. Eat fruits and such foods as raisins/grapes. It can be for a day or even 3 to 5 days. Let your feeling of well-being decide in the long run. Avoid processed foods of all kinds.

Give it a thought. Can you replace this body? No, evidently not! Then I suppose you have no option but to take care of it or be ready to suffer for the neglect. There is no tomorrow really!

Pic of hidden beach thru Susan Jane.

78) Dr PK's Holistic Medico Advisory shared a link.

The world is not thinking for your benefit.

"So, whenever a doctor tells you that you have an incurable or fatal disease, look him squarely in the eye and tell him--- ---! (whatever is your favorite expletive). Then go out and find yourself another doctor- one who believes in the body and not in the disease." --Lawrence Badgley, M.D.

"Over and over I explain to patients, 'Your pain, misery and illness results from your own dietary mistakes and drugs. You are suffering because you are filled with toxic wastes caused by your diet of poorly selected food filled with artificial flavorings, preservatives, synthetics, and over-processed ingredients—too much stimulating food and too few natural vitamins from vegetables and fruits....' "
Henry G. Bieler, MD
Food is Your Best Medicine

Paul Fassa is dedicated to warning others about the current corruption of food and medicine and guiding others toward a direction for better health with no restrictions on health freedom. You can visit his blog at http://healthmaven.blogspot.com/

Health Maven - Escape from the Medical Mafia Matrix

'Drug companies are not here to bring health to the population but to scam them on one level for vast amounts of money, by treating the symptoms and not addressing the cause.'

79) Dr PK's Holistic Medico Advisory

Prostate disorders.

As science continues to shed light on the health benefits associated with eating less meat and more 'earthly' foods like organic fruits and vegetables, more people around the globe are making a transition to a vegetarian and/or vegan diet for a variety of reasons. There is a reason why a plant based diet can help prevent over 60% of chronic disease deaths.

I may also add, that if sex is on your mind and no outlet, then the activated semen has nowhere to go and can infect the prostate & cause cancerous anomalies; if there is pain the groin, then all is not well.

80) Dr PK's Holistic Medico Advisory

Two of my favorite food-cum-snacks that we make at home.
The first one is carrot and milk purée. Grated carrot boiled in whole milk till the only the solids remain in a soft mess. Non refined cane sugar is added when still hot and raisins and nuts added. It is virtually a power packed vitamin/mineral bomb.
The second are cashew nuts roasted in hot rock salt.
Although I love eating plain cashew with raisins too.

 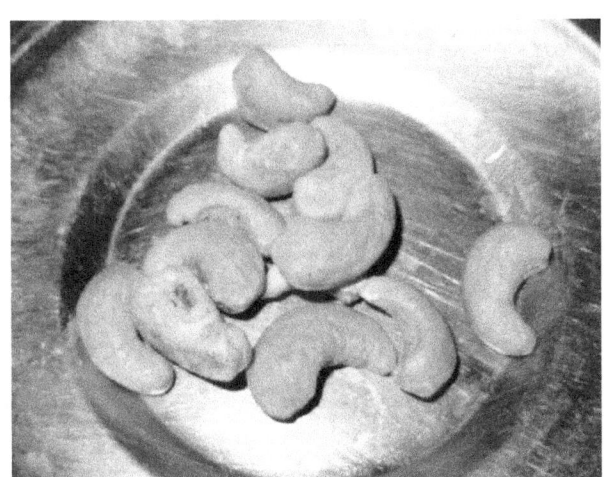

81) Dr PK's Holistic Medico Advisory

Using ice in sprains and bruises.

Ice is best used to help stop blood flow but later on hot and cold compresses help more in recovery by stimulating flow and self-repair by the body by removing damaged cells and stuff and permitting the body to renew the damaged part.
Too much use of ice does the opposite.

The Anecdotal Rationale for Ice:
from Joshua J. Stone, MA, ATC, NASM-CPT, CES, PES, FNS

Somewhere along the line the concept that ice facilitates healing became conventional wisdom. Sorry, that wisdom is wrong. I had someone tell me the other day, "We need to ice, because we need to get the swelling out." Really? Does ice facilitate movement of fluid out of the injured area? No, it does not. The lymphatic system removes swelling. The Textbook of Medical Physiology says it best:

"The lymphatic system is a 'scavenger' system that removes excess fluid, protein molecules, debris, and other matter from the tissue spaces. When fluid enters the terminal lymphatic capillaries, any motion in the tissues that intermittently compresses the lymphatic capillaries propels the lymph forward through the lymphatic system, eventually emptying the lymph back into the circulation."

Lymphatic drainage is facilitated by contraction of surrounding muscle and changes in compressive forces that push the fluid back to the cardiovascular system. This is why ankle pumps works so well and removing swelling accumulation.

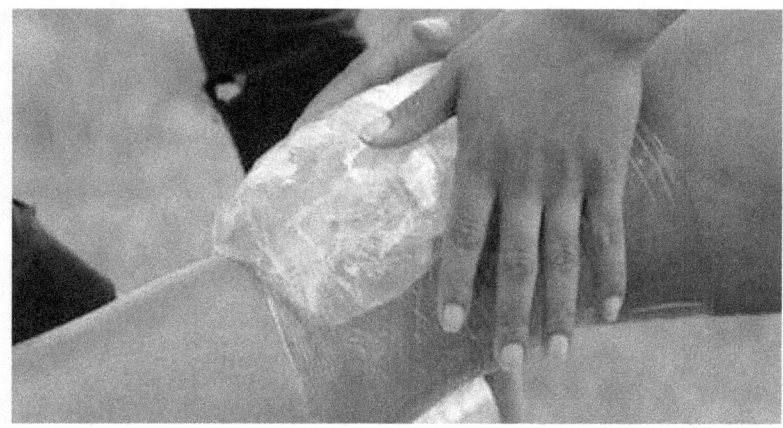

82) Dr PK's Holistic Medico Advisory

Hopscotch is such good exercise. It jingles up the system safely in a safe way and takes your mind off other inanities.

Let everybody of every age join in. And when tired of it, go to skipping.

83) <u>Dr PK's Holistic Medico Advisory</u> shared <u>The Mystic's Quotes</u>'s <u>photo</u>.

It is difficult to influence negatively people who are happy with their selves. They move consciously and deliberately. Their actions are planned and thought-out. Their spirits are in balance with their bodies. So, because they can maintain a modicum level of equanimity, they don't get unduly perturbed and their bodily functions are not distracted or vulnerable to external abuse.
This is the secret of wellness.

People are lonely by selfish tendencies and aloneness is a conscious choice by integrated beings.

84) Dr PK's Holistic Medico Advisory

The bane of too much sitting.

The new culture of office hours and the newer culture of getting everything done with desktop computers has spawned a painful set of bodily problems for which the body was not designed for. Before I say more, I must also admit I don't see when it is a matter of making a living, what other options do we have. But then even when we have free time we are spending long hours in ultra comfortable chairs and sofas and hardly moving at all.
When I look back at my grandfather's place/house, there were no comfortable sitting places. Sleeping was possible but it required getting a cot out from storage and bedding from the store etc and then nobody would leave you alone anyway.
The PDF image below is from:
http://www.washingtonpost.com/wp-srv/special/health/sitting/Sitting.pdf

Don't just sit there!

We know sitting too much is bad, and most of us intuitively feel a little guilty after a long TV binge. But what exactly goes wrong in our bodies when we park ourselves for nearly eight hours per day, the average for a U.S. adult? Many things, say four experts, who detailed a chain of problems from head to toe.

REPORTING BY BONNIE BERKOWITZ; GRAPHIC BY PATTERSON CLARK

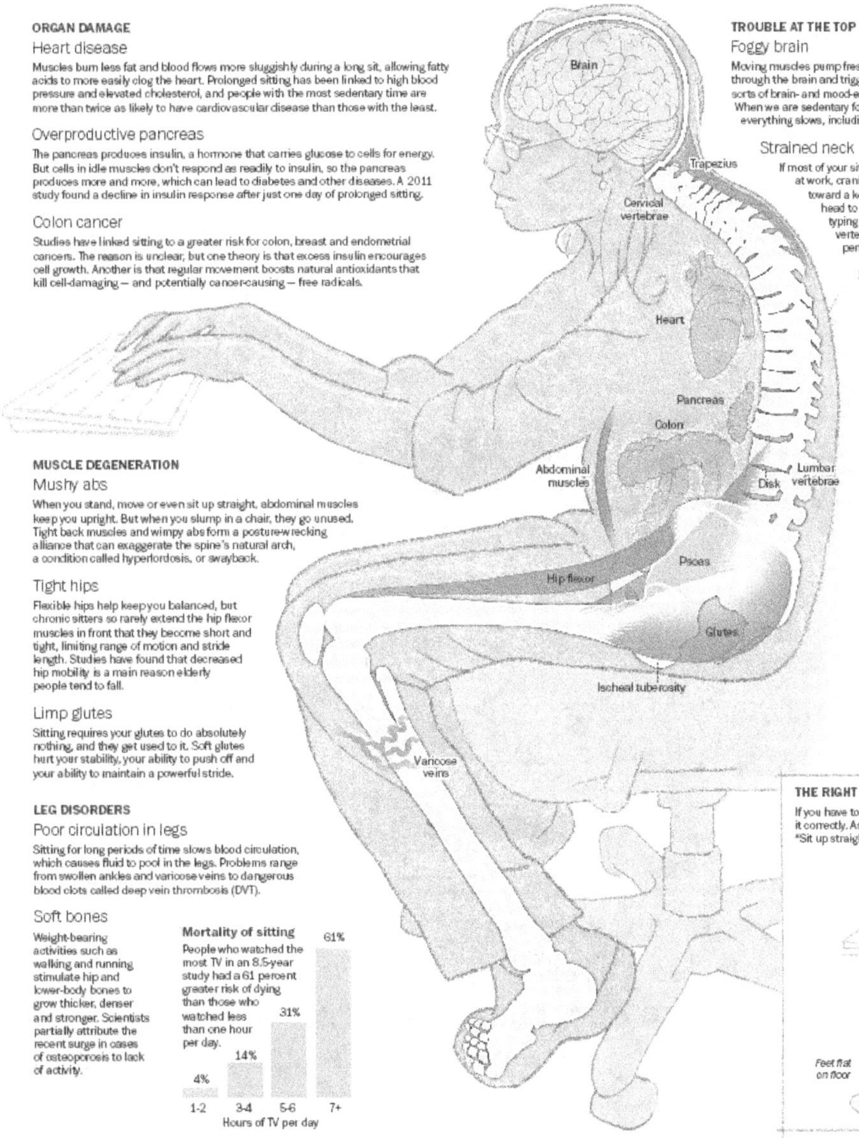

ORGAN DAMAGE

Heart disease

Muscles burn less fat and blood flows more sluggishly during a long sit, allowing fatty acids to more easily clog the heart. Prolonged sitting has been linked to high blood pressure and elevated cholesterol, and people with the most sedentary time are more than twice as likely to have cardiovascular disease than those with the least.

Overproductive pancreas

The pancreas produces insulin, a hormone that carries glucose to cells for energy. But cells in idle muscles don't respond as readily to insulin, so the pancreas produces more and more, which can lead to diabetes and other diseases. A 2011 study found a decline in insulin response after just one day of prolonged sitting.

Colon cancer

Studies have linked sitting to a greater risk for colon, breast and endometrial cancers. The reason is unclear, but one theory is that excess insulin encourages cell growth. Another is that regular movement boosts natural antioxidants that kill cell-damaging — and potentially cancer-causing — free radicals.

MUSCLE DEGENERATION

Mushy abs

When you stand, move or even sit up straight, abdominal muscles keep you upright. But when you slump in a chair, they go unused. Tight back muscles and wimpy abs form a posture-wrecking alliance that can exaggerate the spine's natural arch, a condition called hyperlordosis, or swayback.

Tight hips

Flexible hips help keep you balanced, but chronic sitters so rarely extend the hip flexor muscles in front that they become short and tight, limiting range of motion and stride length. Studies have found that decreased hip mobility is a main reason elderly people tend to fall.

Limp glutes

Sitting requires your glutes to do absolutely nothing, and they get used to it. Soft glutes hurt your stability, your ability to push off and your ability to maintain a powerful stride.

LEG DISORDERS

Poor circulation in legs

Sitting for long periods of time slows blood circulation, which causes fluid to pool in the legs. Problems range from swollen ankles and varicose veins to dangerous blood clots called deep vein thrombosis (DVT).

Soft bones

Weight-bearing activities such as walking and running stimulate hip and lower-body bones to grow thicker, denser and stronger. Scientists partially attribute the recent surge in cases of osteoporosis to lack of activity.

Mortality of sitting
People who watched the most TV in an 8.5-year study had a 61 percent greater risk of dying than those who watched less than one hour per day.

- 61% — 7+
- 31% — 5-6
- 14% — 3-4
- 4% — 1-2

Hours of TV per day

TROUBLE AT THE TOP

Foggy brain

Moving muscles pump fresh blood and oxygen through the brain and trigger the release of all sorts of brain- and mood-enhancing chemicals. When we are sedentary for a long time, everything slows, including brain function.

Strained neck

If most of your sitting occurs at a desk at work, craning your neck forward toward a keyboard or tilting your head to cradle a phone while typing can strain the cervical vertebrae and lead to permanent imbalances.

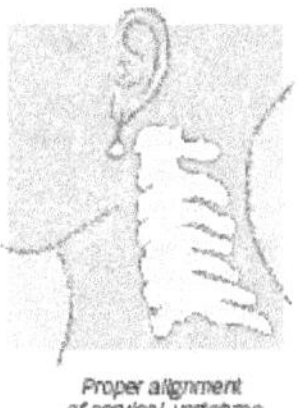

Proper alignment of cervical vertebrae

Sore shoulders and back

The neck doesn't slouch alone. Slumping forward overextends the shoulder and back muscles as well, particularly the trapezius, which connects the neck and shoulders.

BAD BACK

Inflexible spine

Spines that don't move become inflexible and susceptible to damage in mundane activities, such as when you reach for a coffee cup or bend to tie a shoe. When we move around, soft disks between vertebrae expand and contract like sponges, soaking up fresh blood and nutrients. When we sit for a long time, disks are squashed unevenly and lose sponginess. Collagen hardens around supporting tendons and ligaments.

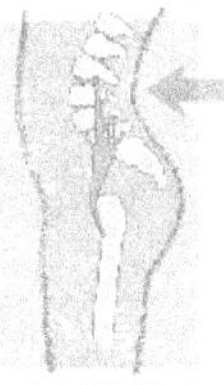

Disk damage

People who sit more are at greater risk for herniated lumbar disks. A muscle called the psoas travels through the abdominal cavity and, when it tightens, pulls the upper lumbar spine forward. Upper-body weight rests entirely on the ischeal tuberosity (sitting bones) instead of being distributed along the arch of the spine.

Lumbar region bowed by shortened psoas

Labels on central figure: Brain, Trapezius, Cervical vertebrae, Heart, Pancreas, Colon, Abdominal muscles, Lumbar vertebrae, Disk, Psoas, Hip flexor, Glutes, Ischeal tuberosity, Varicose veins

THE RIGHT WAY TO SIT

If you have to sit often, try to do it correctly. As Mom always said, "Sit up straight."

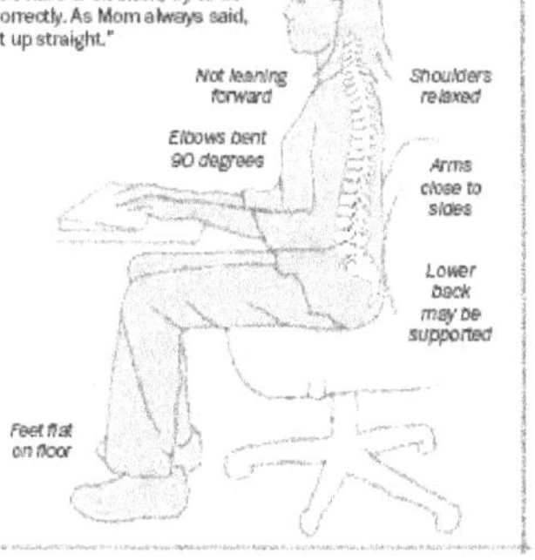

- Not leaning forward
- Shoulders relaxed
- Elbows bent 90 degrees
- Arms close to sides
- Lower back may be supported
- Feet flat on floor

So what can we do? The experts recommend ...

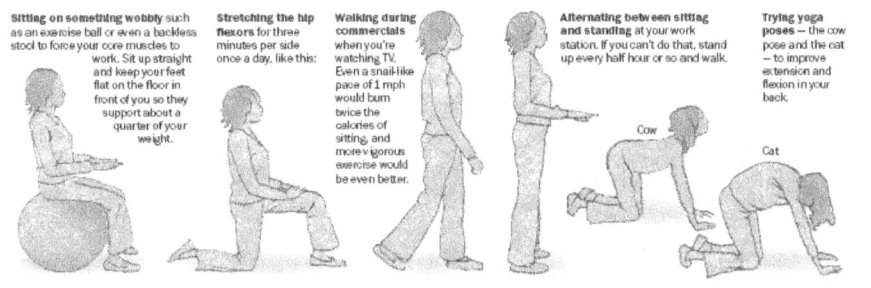

Sitting on something wobbly such as an exercise ball or even a backless stool to force your core muscles to work. Sit up straight and keep your feet flat on the floor in front of you so they support about a quarter of your weight.

Stretching the hip flexors for three minutes per side once a day, like this:

Walking during commercials when you're watching TV. Even a snail-like pace of 1 mph would burn twice the calories of sitting, and more vigorous exercise would be even better.

Alternating between sitting and standing at your work station. If you can't do that, stand up every half hour or so and walk.

Trying yoga poses — the cow pose and the cat — to improve extension and flexion in your back.

Cow

Cat

The experts

Scientists interviewed for this report:

James A. Levine, inventor of the treadmill desk and director of Obesity Solutions at Mayo Clinic and Arizona State University.

Charles E. Matthews, National Cancer Institute investigator and author of several studies on sedentary behavior.

Joy Dicharry, director of the REP Biomechanics Lab in Bend, Ore., and author of "Anatomy for Runners."

Tal Amasay, biomechanist at Barry University's Department of Sport and Exercise Sciences.

Additional sources: "Amount of time spent in sedentary behaviors and cause-specific mortality in U.S. adults," by Charles E. Matthews, et al, of the National Cancer Institute; "Sedentary behavior and cardiovascular disease: a review of prospective studies," by Earl S. Ford and Carl J. Caspersen of the Centers for Disease Control and Prevention; Mayo Clinic.

85) <u>Dr PK's Holistic Medico Advisory</u>

Weight loss.
But why the gain in the first place?

86) Sins of old age

1) Constipation is now a very certain friend. Our lifestyle and foods ensure that we have it. It is not something that can be controlled. Either you have it or you don't. Yu can learn to live with it with purges and laxatives but that does not mean you don't have it.

2) The way to correct the imbalance that constipation creates is by habitually going on intermittent fasts with some natural products like fresh juices, liquefied yogurt.

3) Constipation overloads the elimination process and the lymphatic system. Arthritis/stiff joints, cramps etc are a sign of body asking for relief from the overloads coupled with deficiencies generated over a life time of habits followed – whatever they are.

4) Also take some probiotic preparation that has a multi bacterial mix. Take one capsule 15-20 ms before lunch.
Then before starting lunch, take a small glass of water with a little apple cider vinegar.

5) Women lose nutrients throughout their reproductive cycle that never really get adequately replenished. So: multi vitamin supplements are advised to everybody without exception. A little extra of Vitamin E and B complex will help greatly.
6) Avoid chills.

It is also to be noted that constipation is not just the going to the toilet easily and comfortably. The food has to pass through nearly 50 ft of intestines. If the condition of the intestines is good, with good flora and follicles working at their best, with muscles working well, still the quality of the food if sticky or the kind that putrefies easily, problems can occur.

Gradually with time, a lot of the solids stick to the walls of the intestines and hardens while the core at the center moves. This may give the impression that everything is fine. The truth is that the walls are absorbing toxins from the stuck material which is moving slowly, creating a state of auto-intoxication.

The modern habit of eating 3 good meals a day does NOT give the intestines the time to do their job properly. There is a back log of stupendous size. To this with age is added the problem of weaker muscles, attacks by antibiotics, chills and such. Not well masticated food is downed and weak stomach acid releases not so properly digested stuff into the intestines.

Had it been a man-made machine it would clog away in a few months. The sensible thing to do is to fast and give the body time to take care of itself.

Taking laxatives may give some relief but does not cure or address the problem.

2) The following words were picked
from: http://healthmaven.blogspot.com

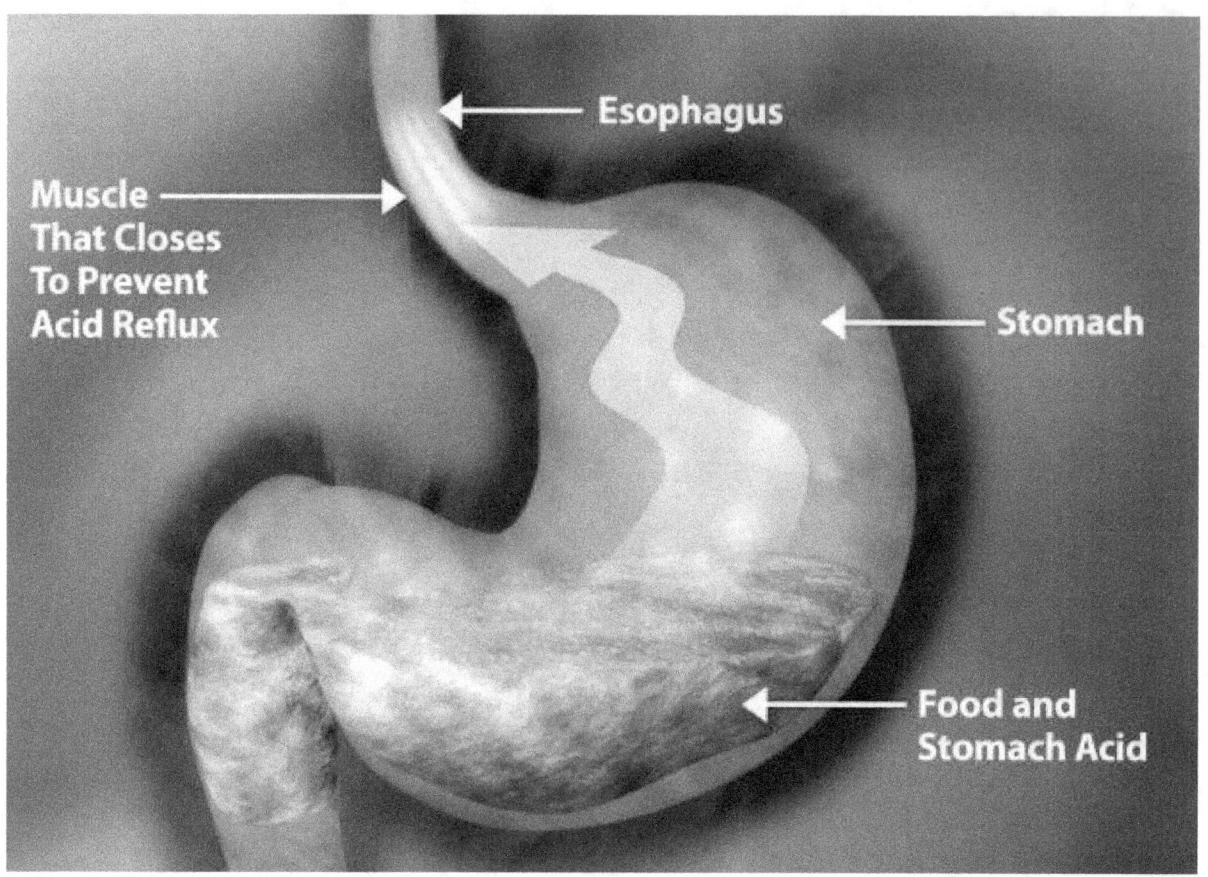

Esophagus

Muscle That Closes To Prevent Acid Reflux

Stomach

Food and Stomach Acid

'Where does it all start? This important question can determine the success or failure of medical treatments so we better get it right. Actually there are several starting places to chronic illness but the one I want to talk about here starts in the stomach, which starts screaming at us with a host of GERD symptoms when things start going wrong in our lives.

One of the most important points for doctors and patients to realize is that GERD is a deficiency disease meaning it is not caused by excess acid- it is caused by deficient acid. When the stomach does not produce enough acid the food sits in the stomach and pushes back up the esophageal sphincter. It is, as they call it an excess acid condition only because it is an acid mix, just not high enough to create proper digestion, but high enough to burn tissues that it is exposed long enough to it.

Hydrochloric acid, referred to as HCl, is produced in the stomach by the parietal cells that lie deep in the stomach walls. The truth is, we wouldn't be able to digest at all without it.

87) Dr PK's Holistic Medico Advisory

On Napping

It was well understood that the most harmful time of the day was the peak of the afternoon. At around midday when the sun is at its peak, the body naturally wants to have a break. If listened to, it will be begging for a nap. Try it. A short nap can be wondrous. It has re-energizing powers, which are undreamt of in today's fast paced world where rest is seen as a dead loss in terms of money if nothing else. Burnout is a reality and beginning to take epidemic proportions. (I have heard people sleep with their phones: what do they have against themselves? Will the world come to a stop? Is the phone for their convenience or the world out there?)

The Hammock by Gustave Courbet

Take medicinal naps.

NAPS KEEP YOU AWAKE.....Let us not forget that we have come from a state of deep sleep and are inching towards another long eternal sleep. So it is safe to assume that sleepiness is our normal state. When on this earth we are required to put in our penny's worth to keep the mother earth going and in return mother earth feeds us. But mother earth understands, therefore she allocated a good night's sleep every 24 hours to keep the connectivity. So we forget at our peril that our aim finally is for a good night's sleep. That is the goal.

WE work, accumulate gold and bricks and create a cozy corner for what? So we can sleep comfortably, undisturbed and uncaring. In the last few generations I wonder where these humans got the idea that they have to work longer periods to be what they call successful. Humans live such topsy-turvy lives.

It is unfortunate that the word siesta has become unfashionable and linked today to laziness. It is in reality related to wisdom. The wise never take their siesta lightly. It is life itself. Try the other way. Think of sleep, doze, nap, siesta as the goal of life.

It is not activity but rest we should live for. All this business of living and earning a living should have for aim to be free from the drudgery of life to be able to take a nap when and where and how we want it. Do you realize that only the truly free and the true master can have this boon?

It's all in the biorhythms. Humans like all other living creatures on our planet sway and swing to a bio-clock. This in layman terms means that there is a cycle to the movement and automatic activities. The flowers open at certain given times only. The cock knows instinctively when to crow. Famous Linnaeus first observed these biorhythms in nature. He even created a garden in which different species of flowers opened and closed at regular but different intervals. So much so that he was able to tell the time by looking at the flowers.

This rhythm also regulates the human metabolism, physiology and behavior. We shouldn't mess too much with this cyclic rhythm. In plain language this works out to something like following the sun in our activities. The body knows what it needs instinctively and we should listen to it.

Lately due to electricity giving us more control on our activity time we have started doing things as and when we please; mostly to the detriment of our health. The first casualty has been sleep in its totality and worse, we now sleep at timings that are at odds with the bio-clock. This is resulting in the metabolism going out of control and the body's own immune system is weakened and the inbuilt regenerative powers are disoriented. Sleep deprivation at its best!

The knowledge imbibed from the past gave us the definitive knowledge about this cycle without understanding the scientific aspects. Necessity of life also made us do the right thing. The sun was our light source and so we compressed all our energies into the sunlight span of the day to make the most of it. Night-time automatically meant unwinding of the system and sleep.

A NAP should be seen as a shot on the arm. Try it instead of a cup of coffee.
Many athletes have reported that they improved their performance when they rested for a day rather than kill themselves by too much practice. The news from Harvard is that the brain continues to learn after furious activity has stopped. It is when it is dozing that it is assimilating what it has been gathering.

88) Dr PK's Holistic Medico Advisory

How to fast and how often?

The idea is to reduce intake of 80-90% of solids. To give time to the food already there to be digested and waste eliminated. You can take grapes, soft fruits, butter milk, even coffee etc. If extremely hungry take a slice of bread but just to kill hunger.

If you have difficulty in remaining hungry start with fasting one day twice a week and then increase the day to two days and later make it 3 days at a stretch at least every 3-4 weeks. But the best is if you could wait for the body to signal that it is not comfortable and feels sluggish or painful in the colon area (where the colon bends, the blockage is max) and gives discomfort at night to result in bad sleep/rest. If your life is sedentary or mostly spent sitting, you need it most.

Once the body gets used to the idea of fasting it will cooperate and will easily go along with you for 3 days or 5 days as the needs be. The first day is always painful – like withdrawal symptoms. Just grin and bear it. When the colon is unblocking itself, dark smelly hard stools will suddenly start plopping out – normally after the 3rd day.

The allergic reactions/symptoms in the body reduce like, itching, sniffling, colds, burning eyes, fatigue, sluggishness etc + BP regularizes.

89) <u>Dr PK's Holistic Medico Advisory</u> shared <u>Business Destination India</u>'s <u>photo</u>.

Care of gums and mouth in general. You must also improve your internal health in general starting with your guts with yoghurt and fruits of all colors to reduce the acidic ph levels in your body.

Traditional Indian tooth-paste = 8-10 drops of mustard oil + Half teaspoon of table salt + a pinch of turmeric; mix into a paste.

You'll never know gum troubles again.

Can be used along with normal commercial toothpaste for greater pleasure in the act of brushing.

90) <u>Dr PK's Holistic Medico Advisory</u> shared <u>Healthy and Natural World</u>'s <u>photo</u>.

When we live in balance and an upset in health occurs, herbs are more than enough to correct the imbalance.

91)   *WATCH YOUR BACK*

Even in those wild days of the Wild West when the gamblers and sharpshooters had a field day, there was one rule, which was never broken, and it was – Watch Your Back.
Most chairs at best are parking slots for the tailbone while the poor spine with its attendant muscles ails away silently.

The spine is the long bone that connects your head to the hips. The ribs are attached to it. The arms and legs are indirectly attached to it also. So in short it is the basic block on which the rest of the structure is dependent. The muscles act as the holding ropes and take all the weight.

126

Talking about the spine, it also acts as the protective conduit for the Spinal Cord, which is the nerve center. Any damage or pressure on it will make us non-functional.

WATCH YOUR BACK (pic of the author of his book)

What causes back pain? The most common causes are sprains and stresses.

Other reasons of back pain are Disc Injury, Osteoarthritis of the spine, Spondylitis, Osteoporosis, Pregnancy etc.

Disc injury creates many problems. The cushion between the vertebras has the tendency to dry-up with age or become weak.

Another common occurrence is osteoarthritis of the spine. It is similar to the defect we see in other joints of the hands and legs and equally painful. Whatever the reason, not bottling up anger and resentment delays its onset and calcium deficiency can be a source. One thing is sure, do not neglect it.

Spondylitis is another of the modern illnesses. The connection to the failure of nutrients in the body resulting in back problems can be a very important point because this problem is seen in many people with Irritable Bowel Disease and Psoriasis. Western medical science may not fully agree but in India due to the influence of naturopathy and Ayurveda, this point is well understood. The absence of exercise in today's modern living and the act of continually sitting in soft chairs, even when traveling has weakened the back structure so much that it is difficult to pinpoint the blame.

Osteoporosis is the result of the bones becoming weaker due to the density being affected, mainly due to lack of minerals. It is seen more in women becomes all throughout their reproductive cycle they lose nutrients, which never really get replaced properly. A little care in this could prevent many unnecessary painful years in old age.

Would you ever believe it? The latest in medical advice is that nine out of ten sufferers of back pain will recover within the first month without any treatment. So my contention that naturopathy can be trusted to give us better advice holds good. All the old and conventional treatments such as traction, corsets, and electrical stimulation though not without merit are now accepted as being generally unhelpful.

When sudden pain occurs due to some injury or physical reason, it would be wise to apply cold packs within the first 48 hours. These would contain the inflammation or bleeding if any within. A pack applied for five minutes at a time with short gaps is ideal. If symptoms last longer than 48 hours then heat fomentation should be continued with. Even a hot shower is advisable. Care is advocated in using heating pads when sleeping as burns may result.

For chronic low back pain, the most important component would be exercise. Study life of today. Half is spent sitting. The lower back muscles simply go limp from disuse and the slightest strain results in an emergency. In today's life style this can be said of all the muscles. Don't forget, the heart is a muscle too.

Well then what about bed rest? Try to get out of it by the third day or most the fourth. Too much bed rest makes the bones lose calcium and weakens the muscles further. Prevention is best. Adopt the practice of aerobic exercises. They are good in every way. Exercise releases endorphins in the body, which are natural painkillers. There is always physiotherapy for acute cases and if discomfort is acute, do not try to do anything without professional advice.

92) Dr PK's Holistic Medico Advisory shared Health & Natural Living's photo.

It such a quirk of fate that now that we can have any kind of food/fruit whenever we want them, we don't want them any more - our preferences are for tasty stale rancid meals and colas. This will go down in history of this earth as the most tragic turn of events.

93)   **Dr PK's Holistic Medico Advisory** shared Health & Natural Living's photo.

Dehydration due to poor water intake is killing more people than any other illness but this fact is sadly not recognised. The instinct of "thirst" has been totally sheeted over by comfortable living. The lack of activity, sweating, and over-intake of other leeching drinks has taken over to the utter destruction of the natural state of health.
Everyone I meet today is suffering and most symptoms show sign of dehydration or lack of lubrication in the body.

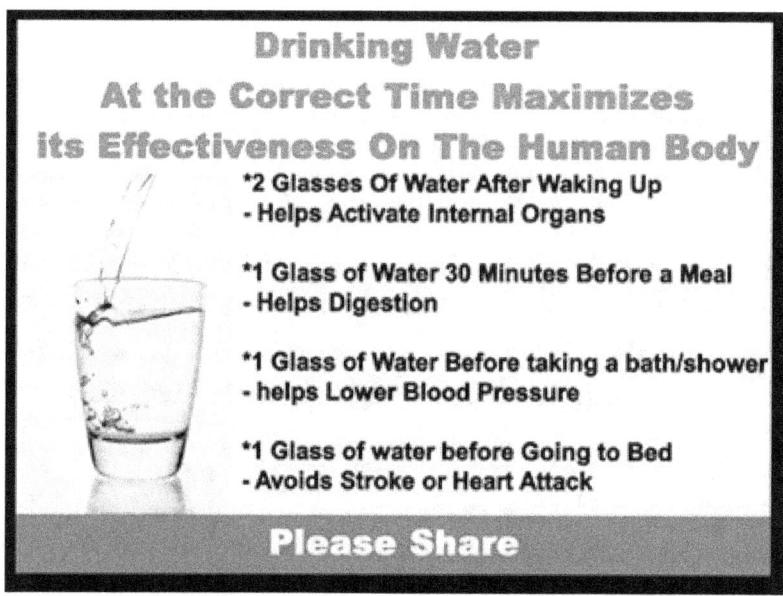

94) Dr PK's Holistic Medico Advisory

The most insidious germ, bacteria, virus or whatever you wish to call it, - is FEAR. It knots (digestion not working, colon getting stuck, blood flow restricted, migraines popping up, cortisone being released and general stress buttons activated etc etc) us up giving us a host of traumas that if allowed to linger will develop into sicknesses and serious diseases. There is enough literature on how fear affects us medically so I won't go into it but it is a factor that we are not computing in our life-styles or accepting it without second thought. Tranquilisers, sleeping potions are not the answer though.

Fear of being forgotten is the biggest fear.

It is also the most natural thing and like death, an absolute truth.

The stupidity or/and understanding of life by the average human is spot-lighted by the concept of the Grave-stone. We just won't let go! We all feel we are worthy to be remembered & listened to and that generations after ours will continue to have any memory of us just because a grave-stone stands out like a sore thumb.

95) Dr PK's Holistic Medico Advisory

I advise using some eye drops to wash the eyes on getting up and going to sleep. The pollution levels today demand this protection. The eyes being the most attacked organ of our body, directly open to attacks with little protection from the elements.

Lubricating eye drops, also known as artificial tears, can provide relief for short-term dry eyes, when the cause is related to temporary circumstances such as computer eye strain, being outdoors in windy and sunny conditions, and tiredness.

Most OTC lubricating eye drops work by adding various tear elements that are in your eyes already, to supplement your natural tears and make your eyes more moist and comfortable.

It's best to avoid decongestant eye drops for dry eye. You'll recognize a decongestant eye drop because it's typically advertised as relief for red eyes.

Decongestants make your eyes look less red, but they also can worsen dry eye symptoms in the long run.

If your dry eye problems are long-term, you may need to use a gel or ointment. Because gels and ointments for dry eyes can cause blurry vision for a while after you put them in your eyes, most people use them just before going to sleep.

96) <u>**Dr PK's Holistic Medico Advisory**</u> shared <u>HealthKart Plus</u>'s <u>photo</u>.

Coconut.
The most complete plant. Every single part of this tree is used and one can live with only this great tree around.

Nutritional Properties
Among the properties of coconut oil, the one which is of greatest interest and the one which we concern ourselves with is about is its nutritional properties. Let us have a look at these.

Medium-Chain Fatty Acids: These saturated fats are the best things that coconut oil has to offer. I know, many of you will raise your eyebrows at the very notion of saturated fats, but believe me, not all saturated fats are bad. These saturated fats are actually medium-chain fatty acids like capric acid, caprylic acid, caproic acid, and lauric acid, which can do wonders for you. They increase the rate of metabolism in your body, thereby aiding in weight loss, increase the level of good cholesterol (high density lipoproteins) and lower the level of bad cholesterol (low density lipoproteins). They are also great sources of energy.

Vitamin-E: This keeps your hair & skin healthy, along with keeping your organic system functioning smoothly, as is done by all vitamins.

Medicinal Properties
Coconut oil is useful in the treatment of a number of medical conditions, some of which are explained in greater detail below.

Cures fatigue: The saturated fats present in coconut oil, being great source of energy, effectively cure fatigue and energy malnutrition.

Antioxidant and Anti-Aging Properties: The antioxidant properties of Coconut oil come from its saturated fats like Capric Acid, Caprylic Acid, Caproic Acid, and Myristic Acid. They counter adverse effects of ageing, macular degeneration, whitening of hair, and sagging of the skin.

Antimicrobial Properties: The acids discussed above convert themselves into great antimicrobial and anti-fungal agents like monocaprin and monolaurin when acted upon by certain enzymes. These derivatives protect our body, both internally and externally, from conditions like Athlete's Foot, rashes, itches, ringworm, and dermatitis.

Reduces Hair Loss: This property of Coconut oil is the most famous, at least in India and on the Indian Subcontinent. It keeps hair black, prevents it from whitening and hair loss.

Candida: The antimicrobial properties of Coconut oil, discussed above, have been found to be effective against Candida.

Vermifuge: Coconut oil can be used against intestinal round worms and tape worms.

Dandruff: It prevents peeling away of the skin on the scalp and conditions like dandruff by keeping the skin moist and smooth.

Digestive Disorders: This oil, taken regularly in proper quantity, can help cure chronic digestive problems.

Cancer: The saturated fatty acids, discussed above, help protect against many types of cancer. These are the same fatty acids that are found in Mother's milk.

HIV: Quite recently, some rays of hope have been seen while using Coconut oil against the HIV infection, again due to the presence of those fatty acids.

Blockage in the Arteries: The Medium-chain triglycerides present in Coconut oil lower the level of bad cholesterol and help clear blockages, thereby reducing the risk of heart attacks. Thus, despite all the negative comments against Coconut oil due to its saturated fats, it is actually cardiac friendly.

Cracking of Skin: Coconut oil is undoubtedly the best skin care agent you can use. That being said, a small amount of people are allergic to coconut oil, and can show irritation. Its stability, antimicrobial properties, moisture retaining capacity, and ability to solidify below 24o C makes it an ideal protective agent against cracking of the skin. Vitamin-E adds to this property immensely.

Obesity: Coconut oil speeds up the metabolic activities and thus burning of fats in the body, resulting in weight loss.

Other properties: Coconut oil is found to help absorption of fat-soluble vitamins and glucose in the body, aid proper secretion of insulin, improve circulation and fight tumors, colitis, ulcers in the stomach and food pipe, correct renal infections, reduce inflammation due to rashes or contact with foreign substances. It is also very effective in curing and relieving bruises and small cuts.

(from: http://www.organicfacts.net/organic-oils/properties-of-coconut-oil.html)

97) Dr PK's Holistic Medico Advisory

In my experience, 3 out of 5 coughs nowadays are due to acidosis. In this a decoction of aniseed(saunf), and ajwain (Bishops's weed) works or even using honey + Avipatikar churna.
The most effective product has always been honey.

COUGH REMEDIES

Honey, onion and garlic syrup

Combine a half-cup of honey and a half-cup of water. Add in one whole chopped onion and one chopped clove of garlic. Add a dash of sage, thyme or oregano and allow to steep overnight at room temperature. Strain and use the liquid as a cough syrup. Store in your refrigerator.

98) Dr PK's Holistic Medico Advisory shared <u>Pachamama</u> <u>Alliance</u>'s <u>photo</u>.

Trees, woods, gardens, parks are medicine.
This is why I suppose we, when we are with trees, we regain our positivity, recoup our strength, get back our sparkle, feed well on vegetarian fare and sloth drops off like a useless old coat.

Forest bathing
"The Japanese term Shinrin-yoku may literally mean "forest bathing," but it doesn't involve soaking in a tub among the trees. Rather it refers to spending time in the woods for its therapeutic (or bathing) effect. Most of us have felt tension slip away in the midst of trees and nature's beauty. But science now confirms its healing influence on the body. When you spend a few hours on a woodland hike or camping by a lake you breathe in phytoncides, active substances released by plants to protect them against insects and from rotting, which appear to lower blood pressure and stress and boost your immune system." ~Mother Nature Network

99) *Survival is at stake - wake up.*

The astonishing human race leaves me dumfounded at every turn. The brilliance of their minds is really worthy of greatness but they decided, except for some individuals, to abdicate their entire rights to govern, think, eat & drink, love, fraternize and everything else.
Even their Gods are conceptualized for them with little or no personal touch.
After eons, the concept of democracy arrived, the spread of education happened, knowledge for every-day living &possibilities for bettering one's lot was now at one's finger-tips but all that these humans did was to abdicate their rights to live in an illusionary little cocoon for their tiny pleasure which as we can clearly see are now being taken away from them one by one.
Now as we speak, the democratically elected kings are more worried to amass wealth in the short span they are in the chair, the industry is pouring out products that give us convenience and comfort but take away our health and the humans still think it is all for their good. And spiritual independence and avarice has given free reign to con artists who are showing us the way to heaven while they go stuffing their bank accounts. The food and medical industry is selling us dreams and digging our graves.
The sheeples are content and ready to spend their time at spas and golf courts fashioned from devastated forests. The question is how long will this activity of devastation last? Soon there will be more poison in the air, water and earth than nutrients; how shall we survive?

100)   Temporary relief.

Yesterday, I was passing by and over-heard my neighbor talking to another: Why have you stopped the pain killers?
And the neighbor replied sagely: What's the use? It was not making me any better.

And this struck me how easily we forget that pain killers are just that
- kill the pain; NOT curative medicine. Killing the pain won't make it

go away. The sickness needs to be attended to!

Similarly I am seeing abuse of antacids and antihistamines.

People, friends, please top this. These are all emergency medications. They cannot be seen as cures. They actually leave you more debilitated as they burden the body with elimination process that leeches out many other nutrients or poisons the body in some other way.

For example: Antacids contain aluminum hydroxide – not good.

Abuse of prescription painkillers is a "growing, deadly epidemic," according to the Centers for Disease Control and Prevention.

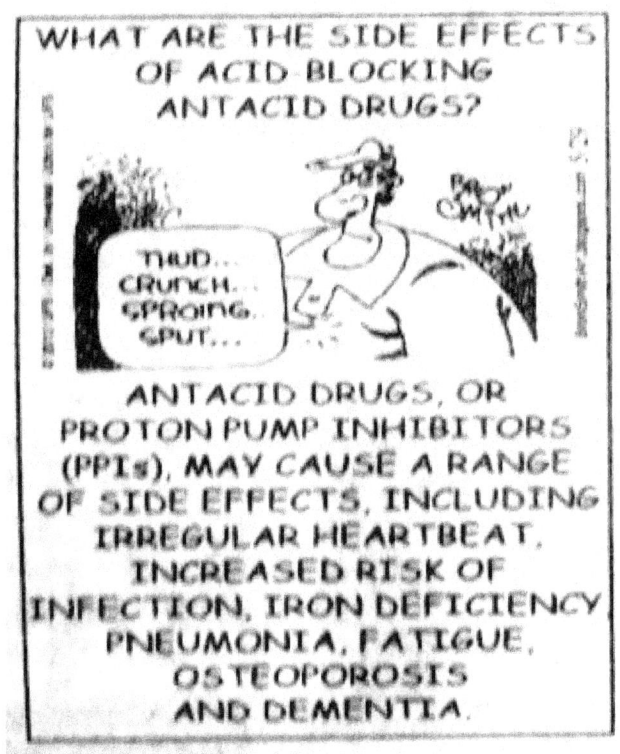

101) Dr PK's Holistic Medico Advisory

When, How & How much to eat?

The advice going around is that one should start with a good breakfast. It looks more like advertising by the cereal makers.

We should eat when the body signals and never by the clock. Most people nowadays eat well at night, so they are not hungry in the morning. My advice is: take your time. And if the hunger pangs are not acute, don't eat. But drink some good nutritious stuff or opt for fruits – this will do more good than bacon and eggs or cornflakes.

There was a time when people slept with the sun and woke up with it. They worked hard physically in the fields and factories or even in the office with out too many stops or luxuries.

This scene has totally changed.

The dining and sleeping times have changed drastically and waking up times along with the times of the morning toilet has changed. The kind of food and quantity of it has also changed.

The entire process of digesting and assimilation and elimination has seen a sea change - not for the better unfortunately.

We are ingesting way too much in one 24 hour cycle over longer periods than the day-time hours and giving it less time to be fully processed. The elimination process time has been reduced. The intestines & colon is being given stuff over and above its capacity to process within the time reduced time frame. It is stifling and suffocating under the onslaught.

The tragedy is that people are satisfied with symptomatic relief. Of course when one is pain that is all one wants.

But once there is relief, they tend to ignore any festering problems. They are not looking for cures. Analgesics, antacids, antipyretics, antispasmodics, aspirin/paracetamol preparations, steroids, sleeping pills, antidepressants, cough suppressants, laxatives, braces and now in cosmetics things like sweat-suppressants etc... etc; does this sound like an intelligent humanity in search of good health?

When you dont' have a healthy diet, medicine will never be of use to correct your health problems. When you have a healthy diet, there is no need for medicine.

A weak constitution cannot support anything. I have seen operations being performed on terminal cases. It is criminal. The operation only speeds up the race to death; it may prolong it for a while in great pain but in the final analysis only enriches the medical establishment. Reminds me of Voltaire's quote where he talks of doctors who know little, pouring medicines that they know even less about in the human body of which they know nothing: Curing the disease and killing the patient.

"Medicines are of subordinate importance because of their very nature they can only work symptomatically." ~ Hans Kusche, M.D.

103) <u>Dr PK's Holistic Medico Advisory</u> shared <u>Skai Juice's</u><u>photo</u>.

Considering the dehydration levels and the reduced intake of chlorophyll in our lives this formula should do wonders. Technically it should activate the lymphatic drainage, activate the kidneys, wash the liver and rumble-up the intestines.

I'm open to this! FREE WELLNESS GUIDE: <u>www.skaijuice.com</u>

Some people do not get sick – why?

It's tempting to dismiss it as luck: Some people might catch a slight cold or suffer an occasional ache or pain now and then, but they never seem to suffer from flus, fevers and illnesses that send the rest of us diving under the covers for days.
Here are 8 surprising habits of those people who never get sick — and how you can adapt them to your own soon-to-be healthier life.

1. THEY STRESS LESS Stress damages the immune system and the heart. There's also evidence that learning relaxation techniques early on is crucial: like meditation or sitting quietly by the river.

2. THEY EAT LESS They don't gorge- whatever the temptation.

3. THEY OPT FOR HERBAL REMEDIES. Although plant-based health aids have been long derided by the Western medical community.

4. THEY MAKE FRIENDS A PRIORITY Studies show that people with strong friendships tend to have more robust immune systems and are less likely to succumb to infectious diseases. The support system counts.

5. THEY STAY Ph BALANCED the body is healthiest when its systems are functioning midway i.e., pH balanced

6. THEY EAT GARLIC and other stuff like turmeric etc

7. THEY DETOX REGULARLY (Dr PK: read my advice on intermittent fasting) Many chemicals used commonly today—such as phthalates, dioxins and PCBs—were absent from our environment a century ago. That might be why the rates of diseases (including cancer and liver disease) linked to toxic exposures are increasing.

8. THEY TAKE MORE NAPS Sleep deprivation has the same biological effect as stress: Overtired bodies ratchet up production of the hormone

cortisol, which gives you energy but restricts production of human growth hormone, limiting your body's ability to repair itself. Just like stress, sleep loss has a degenerative effect on your health, and lack of sleep is also tied to compromised immune function.

(This write-up was picked (edited by me) from the internet, I don't remember where. Pic thru my FB friend Fatima Massole)

105) Dr PK's Holistic Medico Advisory

Manipulative cunning doesn't pay – neither health-wise nor in the pragmatic world.

This question merits attention from the holistic point of view.

Although it is difficult to perceive it as directly related to health by the general populace, it is one of the main reasons for our ailments.
HOW AWARE ARE YOU ABOUT YOUR TENDENCIES in trying to be clever or cunning or manipulative.
Manipulative thoughts can permeate every single wish that births in us. They in turn create worries when not in tune with reality. Our wishes and desire are behind it all. When things are not going as we desire we

become tense. AND this is the beginning of a negative wave that can make us really sick. This is within us.

The world outside us is not stupid. They see the selfishness or it will eventually become apparent to everybody one of these days. This then hurts your own future as friendly support in personal or/and professional life dwindles away. Financial losses are a definite possibility.

This gives rise to depression and desperation; enough to make anyone really sick.

But things can go further. In a morose state of mind we can make life-threatening mistakes (like when driving) and in desperation take highly risky decisions that can utterly ruin our lives – even end it.

106) Dr PK's Holistic Medico Advisory

Choose experience over qualifications and shiny clinics.

Dr Pk:
When somebody is treating me I don't want somebody just out of school. I want somebody who is knowledgeable, preferably with a multi disciplinary approach and knowledge and honest enough to agree if he is not sure. Then leaves it to me to google and mess up my life!

There is a saying in India: Don't go to a Vaid(doctor) less than 40 years of age.

144

Edward Stanulevich IV:
I would rather have someone who doesn't think they know everything than someone who is so delusional that they think they do!
The best physicians I have seen never claim to know everything. They know what they know and work with that. What they aren't sure of they look up. If it is beyond their experience or expertise, they refer you to a physician with more experience with your issues.

Contessa Miller:
Yes, PK, it puts the responsibility of caring for OUR bodies, minds, spirits squarely upon our shoulders. We can always use help from others, including doctors, on specific things, but the ultimate care of our bodies rests upon us.

107) Dr PK's Holistic Medico Advisory

Therapeutically speaking.

Get out. Leave your encroaching walls. Far away from the goring eyes of neighbors and crowds.
Then when you come to this spot, lie down and sleep the day away irresponsibly. A multi-pill: tranquiliser, anti-depressant, rejuvenating, opening you to the intuitive world and creative ideas - bringing clarity and solutions; giving your body a chance to rediscover itself.
Pic from Gary Edward Jennings. Some of Mary's work...

108) Dr PK's Holistic Medico Advisory

Essentials Oils bring the awesome power of flowers and plants in a concentrated form to us - in a simple easy-to use product. They are not used much because they are expensive and not always immediately effective like aspirins. But the same products in homeopathic preparations have miraculous results.

There are many essential oils for pain relief, and people who use them seem to heal more quickly than others. Some essential oils have analgesic properties, which means they have shown to relieve or reduce pain, as well as they are anti-spasmodic, anti-inflammatory and anti-rheumatic properties.
Excerpts taken from: http://www.healthyandnaturalworld.com/essential-oils-to-relieve-pain/

Important note - some essential oils are not suitable for pregnant women or people with certain medical conditions. Check with your doctor before using them.

1. Chamomile - is well known for its effective anti-inflammatory properties. Helps to relieve muscle pain and spasms, low back pain, headaches and pain caused by PMS.
2. Sweet marjoram – has sedative properties. Helps to relieve muscle pain and spasms, stiffness, rheumatism, osteoarthritis and migraine.
3. Lavender – this is probably the most famous essential oil for pain relief and relaxation. It has anti-inflammatory, anti-microbial and sedative properties and it helps to relieve muscle tension and spasms, joint pain and headache.
4. Eucalyptus – has analgesic and anti-inflammatory properties. Good for muscle pain and nerve pain. Use in small quantities.
5. Peppermint – good for muscle and joint pain, headache and nerve pain.
6. Rosemary – has analgesic and antispasmodic properties. Good for relieving back pain, muscle and joint pain and headaches.

7. Thyme – antispasmodic, good for joint and muscle pain as well as backache.

8. Clary sage – has calming and soothing properties, as well as anti-spasmodic and anti-inflammatory properties. Helps to ease muscle tension, spasms and PMS pain. Use in small quantities.

9. Sandalwood – relieves muscle spasms. One of sandalwood's most important uses is to sedate the nervous system, so it helps to reduce nerve pain.

10. Juniper – has antispasmodic properties. Relieves nerve pain, joint and muscle aches and spasms.

11. Ginger – can ease back pain and improves mobility. Can be used to treat arthritic and rheumatic pain, muscle pain and sprains.

12. Frankincense – has anti-inflammatory properties and also acts as a mild sedative. It's also used to alleviate stress and relieve pain.

13. Yarrow – a powerful restorative and analgesic pain reliever with powerful anti-inflammatory properties. Good for muscle and joint aches and pains.

14. Wintergreen – this is not a well known essential oil, but it's very effective to treat painful conditions including headache, nerve pain, arthritis and menstrual cramps. This essential oil is created by steam distilling the leaves, and it contains a very high percentage of methyl salicylate. This oil has pain-relieving properties similar to aspirin (salicylate is the principal component of aspirin).

15. Vetiver – not very known in the west, vetiver has been used since ancient times in Ayurvedic medicine. Vetiver essential oil is extracted from the roots of a grass known as Vetiveria zizanoides which belongs to the same botanical family as lemongrass and citronella. It brings relief to general aches and pains, especially for rheumatism, arthritis and muscular pain and headache.

How to use the essential oils to relieve pain?
While you can use any of these oils on their own, it is also beneficial to blend up to three oils together. Don't apply essential oils directly on the skin, but dilute it first with a carrier oil such as olive oil, jojoba oil, sweet almond oil, etc.

109) <u>Dr PK's Holistic Medico Advisory</u>

The cleansing and baths!

Once in a while, we should permit the dead skin & muck to be properly washed away. Open the pores etc. I would not advise using harsh soaps or/and the anti-bacterial kind.

My experience is that unless the head has felt water, the body does not react to the feeling of freshness.

I love a bath but don't like showers. It is waste of water and hot water composed of chlorine and things come at high speed, overwhelming the face, head and breathing; this cannot be a good idea.

I don't agree with too long bath-tub soaks either – specially in hot water. I did it once and then I found that I could not get out of the bath and it took me all my will power to reach the bed where I stayed for 2 hours before my over-heated body cooled down and my brain regained its composure.

110) Dr PK's Holistic Medico Advisory

Long back, I remember reading that to maintain optimum health in old age, after the age of 35-40; we should start losing weight by the average of 200gms per year - based on the optimum average weight.
But this traditionally thinking has been totally junked and the opposite is more apparent.
The reality is that most people today need to shed double this at least.
In our times now where cars are better understood than health and people, I am reminded of my first small Japanese car that I loved for its reliable and smooth functioning. But with age it could not take the extra weight of two in the back. Gradually the entire structure became rotten. I just couldn't bear to part with it but after marriage my wife refused to sit in it as the bottom started falling out.
Like-wise in life we need to learn to give up eating for pleasure, throw away habits that are hurting or face the consequences without complaining. This is called maturing and no amount of ignoring will make it go away.

111) Dr PK's Holistic Medico Advisory sharedsmartsearch.ie's photo.

For some the conditions are never right. Their litany of complaints never ceases. The heartburn they cause and depression they spread around seems to be their primary motive to be alive. These are acid beings and joy and contentment can never be where they are. Good health is simply not possible in these biting conditions.

Yet, give them something that they want and for a moment they become supremely nice. They are so obviously simple and see-through.

112) *Relax, Energise, Forge ahead*

Anti-stressing– sleeping well.

Don't just keep going on and on. That is the route to burn –outs & and low efficiency and errors.
The mantra should be Recline, Decline, Sublime.
1) First recline. Let the body find its most comfortable position.
2) Decline the thoughts that come to you asking for attention. Instead try to picture a huge blackboard and focus on the black. If the thoughts stray, come back to it.
3) Sublimate your positive feelings. Count your blessings and look within for your feelings that are irritating you. Help yourself grow-up with re-enforcement from your library of quotes/quotations that have touched your spirit earlier (a small library I feel we should all have; that we should visit regularly).

What else?

Think less and do.

Too heavily thought out acts keep us back & make us miss the bus to greater things. Aim for spontaneity. That is the genuine yearning of the soul.

It is in doing that the doors open; not in safe secure & fenced in living.

It is my experience that everything I did in my life, every act, talent acquired, finally came in handy at some point in life. - Or shall I say that the opportunity became available because I was prepared?

Nobody believes in being prepared. They will learn to swim only when thrown into the water.

In India we say: They will run to dig a well when the fire has started!

It may be the information age but nobody is reading or bothering to inform oneself. Perseverance is weakening and tempers shortening. It is a sad age. There is much to read, easily available but lesser number of people are actually bothering to make the effort to read – they are happy with the pictures and a few headlines.

We need to spend energies to reflect and introspect.

I see whole lives spent in policing others. Looking for faults and getting irritated and irritating others. Just so any focus from oneself can be avoided. And then feel superior as well.

Things are what they are. First we need to accept. No point in taking a superior, holier than thou attitude.

There are more preachers than students.

Do we really know what the best is for us?

113) Ginger

wow - you know one of our favorites is sliced ginger with lemon, allowed to stand for an hour. Yesterday I finished off one small plate of it with my bread.   Scientists Find Ginger Kills 91% Of Leukemia Cells And Shrinks Tumors In Vivo:

http://www.herbs-info.com/blog/scientists-find-substance-ginger-kills-leukemia-cells-shrinks-tumors-vivo/

114) <u>Dr PK's Holistic Medico Advisory</u> shared <u>Alexander Jansson</u>'s <u>photo</u>.

This picture really makes me think about my life and how small is the circle in which I move and really need.
But what grand postures we enact - pushing the body over the cliff without which we are but a tomb-stone.

115) <u>Dr PK's Holistic Medico Advisory</u>

Want to live happily ever after.
Share your life. Pass it on. Enjoy the company of children and share the awe. Specially the awe even if you know it all. Try to share the awe of newness with real involvement in the game wholeheartedly.

Painting by P P Rubens.

The Power Walk.

To renergise your system. Walk at a continuous speed – whatever speed you are comfortable in. Move the hands back forth in a small arc with hands half-cupped. Keep your eyes glued to the road about 2 meters away. Try to keep a regular unwavering speed – a little brisk if you can. Pull in your tummy and keep it there. Breathe normally. Keep your mind on your walk, breathing and if the tummy is pulled in or not. Just go on and on till your lusting for a cup of coffee becomes just too much. Then rush home. Do at least 2 kms out and 2 back. Any time of the day when the temperature is comfortable is OK. Avoid polluted areas because you would imbibe much negativity from the concentrated ions that sap energy.
Absolute no-no: No talking. Not even thinking if you can manage it.

154

117)   How well are you sleeping?

Your state of health shows more at the time of sleep. Specially when you are waking up. How do you feel then will point to your shortcomings in health. For example, do your eyes open with discomfort? Is your throat dry? Are your joints stiff? Did you really sleep or snooze in short stints? Any problems with sour eructations? Pain around the colon? Do you get cramps pr limbs going to sleep?
How easily do you go to sleep and what all wakes you up or disturbs you? What is the best sleep-time of the day's 24 cycle when you feel fully energized and always sleep well, deeply even though for a short period?
Poor-quality sleep along with frequent awakenings accelerates cancer growth
A new study has revealed that poor-quality sleep marked by frequent awakenings can speed cancer growth, increase tumour aggressiveness and dampen the immune system's ability to control or eradicate early cancers. "Fragmented sleep changes how the immune system deals with probable diseases taking root in the body in ways that make the disease more aggressive," study director David Gozal, MD, chairman of paediatrics at the University of Chicago Comer Children's Hospital, said.

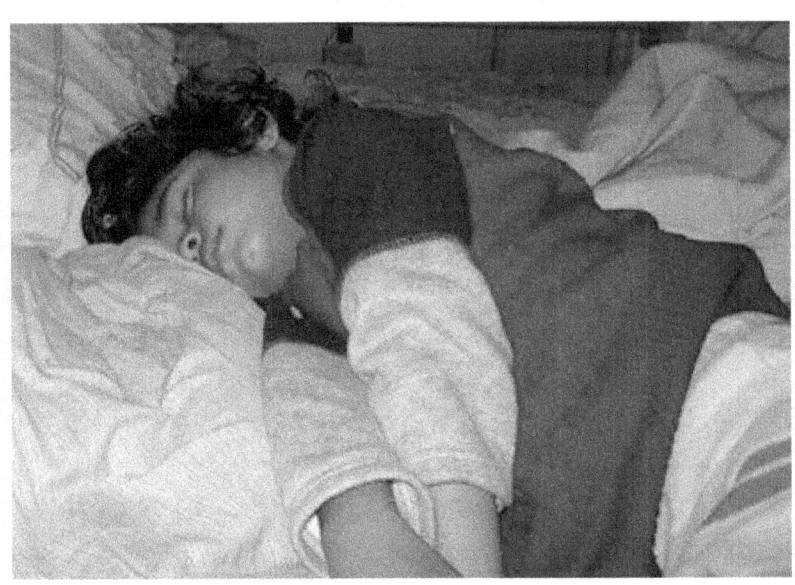

118) Dr PK's Holistic Medico Advisory

Eating coarser grains makes it easy on the intestines to move the load and process it.
Millets: Coarser grains like Millet (ragi), Sorghum/Milo(jowar), and Pearl millet (bajra) are high on fiber-content and great for controlling cholesterol and melting fat.

119) Dr PK's Holistic Medico Advisory shared Dr. Judith Orloff's photo.

More often than not our sicknesses are results of adamant stances. When our wishes and the "doings" of the Universe are not in great accord. We want to stay put, the Universe wants to push ahead; we want nothing to change and the Universe has already changed and gone ahead. We are naturally at logger-heads with life and our body suffers from the inertia and consequences.
Surrender to water and be like water. Flow around obstacles. "The Ecstasy of Surrender." I love this sand art!!!!!!

120) Dr PK's Holistic Medico Advisory

TOMORROW NEVER COMES

You know things are not right. You need to reduce weight, or eat less sugar or drink less alcohol or sleep more or drink more water and full home-made meals.

But do we?

When we are sick we promise ourselves that we shall definitely implement our resolve from the next day. Does the next day ever come?

It is an undeniable fact that we are set in our patterns of thinking, feeling and living. We mat rationalize it anyway we want, but we are surely not for change although we may talk and philosophise/sermonize endlessly.

There was a song in the movie Yellow Rolls Royce, which affected me deeply. It says, "Let's forget about domani, for domani never comes."

121) Asthma update

Asthma is a knee-jerk reaction of the body to acidosis from within and allergic reactions to pollutants and chemicals from without.
Its manifestation can be reduced considerably by taking care to
1) Never get constipated naturally (this does not include controlling it by laxatives)
2) Avoid dust and fumes and strong smells from cooking, engine exhausts, workplaces etc
3) Avoid getting chilled in cold weather. Protect the wind-pipe from chills.
4) Avoid foods that cause indigestion. Combination of raw foods + alcohol is absolute poison. Artificially processed foods and additives are taboo.

Asthma's roots are psychologically in an over-sensitive, easily irritated persona- even a little dogmatic. Somebody who has had a not-so-loving childhood is highly prone to it.
The capacity of the lungs to absorb oxygen is low in asthma and vitamin E is always deficient in these patients. A good supplement of Vits A,D,E and C can improve greatly the resistance.
By increasing the efficiency of digesting and assimilation one reduces the acidosis and auto-intoxication. B vitamins and probiotics are recommended. When the lymphatic system is not blocked or over-loaded the body is able to manage better and avoid attacks.

Some more pointers:

Only an asthmatic knows the suffering of another asthmatic.
The first and most important is that patients tend to take asthma rather casually. Unfortunately the same can also be said for their doctors, which is rather shocking.

The incidence of asthma is increasing worldwide. Nobody wants to put his reputation at stake and agree that what is suspected is behind this increase. But almost everybody agrees that it is the greater exposure to allergens, immune-system imbalances and other difficulties like obesity that are at its root. The city dwellers are the worst affected.

Other protective steps that you can take to prevent triggers are:

1) Keep a clean allergen-proof home. Animals are a potential hazard and should be avoided. Dust mites are very serious allergens. Aerate your house with fresh air everyday. Use exhaust fans if needed.

2) Avoid air-conditioners and cold spaces. Air conditioners have the double disadvantage of creating fungal spores in ducting and creating cold weather artificially that can also trigger chest complications. If you have to, wear some protective clothing to protect your chest from exposure to cold that can give you spasms.

3) Smoking has to be a no-no; whatever are the reasons. In your life it has to go and never tolerate second had smoke under any circumstances. Wood smoke, incense sticks, spices being curried can trigger off almost immediately.

4) Foods also need to be kept on check. There are many foods that can trigger discomfort. Most asthmatics know which food affects them and they should not risk themselves for the pleasure of taste.

5) Don't exhaust yourself in exercise. You need to conserve all the oxygen your body has. When the lungs are not doing their job well, go slow on physical activity.

6) Don't be afraid to take the new combination drugs now available. The side effects are nothing compared to the benefits derived from the inhalers. When using inhalers, rinse your mouth after use.

7) Avoiding congested roads where concentrations of obnoxious substances is very high is highly recommended; especially in open cars or transport that allows the polluted air to go straight into the lungs at high speeds – specially when you are talking in these conditions.

Preserve Planet's photo. (these are the kind of places that are heaven to asthmatics.)

122) Dr PK's Holistic Medico Advisory shared Caregiver Resource Inc's photo.

One of my most loved foods. In summers, it can be a life saver. I often eat one whole cucumber for lunch with cold buttermilk and nothing else. The best thing to do when coming in from exposure in the sun when the temperatures are above 40 deg C.
Winter, Spring, Summer, or Fall.... Don't forget the benefits of cucumbers. Ounce for ounce, they are one of the best veggies that can change the body pH to alkaline.
It is great food to make you feel full and easy to eat. It is a versatile little thing. Much on it, sandwich it, juice it, and grate it – whatever.

A boon for people on fast and aiming to reduce food intake.

Health Benefits of Cucumbers

- reduces the swelling around the eyes
- diuretic
- expel toxins from the digestive system
- promote joint health
- expel tapeworms
- rich in silica content
- reduce uric acid
- Treat sore teeth and gums
- cure diabetes
- 90 percent water

RawForBeauty.com

123) A new morning

A new morning and there is much muck to wash off. The weight of all these apprehensive thoughts is weighing heavy. The mind is in turmoil, searching for way out of the enigmas.

The mind can only work with the info it has and clearly what it has is not enough.

So we are required to learn more and renew our "connect" with the Universe. Is our courage upto it? Will our laziness agree to move? The mind is the instrument that helps us grow and it is also the instrument that argues against new adventures and learning. Its laziness permeates our being and the body has to suffer for it.

124) Dr PK's Holistic Medico Advisory
shared PreventDisease.com's photo.

This is to be recommended: Nature's Flu Shot
http://preventdisease.com/news/14/013114_Natures-Flu-Shot.shtml

There is no value in a flu vaccine because it does not work with the body to facilitate prevention or healing--it works against it. There is also no evidence of any benefit of flu shots due to the vast majority of industry-funded trials which are highly inadequate. Nature has the ultimate flu shot with pure, ultra immune boosting power that a vaccine can never match. This recipe stimulates the immune system to such an extent, that people often report results within as little as three hours.

Works equally well in Colds, stuffed noses and sinusitis, sore-throats. Start treatment at the very first signs and repeat as often wanted.

125) Gall stones.

Danny Jewell to Dr PK's Holistic Medico Advisory
What is the best thing to take in order to remove Gallstones?

Dr PK's Holistic Medico Advisory

Gall stones are formed when the bile that should have been used does not get used up and distributed and dries up in the gallbladder. Once the stones are formed, it is like caramelisation or cement getting set. Very difficult to break it up or dissolve although reversing any serious formations like these is a possibility if pursued (there are always means in nature) but in normal conditions I wouldn't risk giving advice in general.
This is something that comes from family eating habits that are also passed on genetically. Often high density fats, over-fried food and such difficult to digest foods in great quantities right from childhood are mostly responsible. Once the liver, intestines etc are all fatigued and galls stones have formed, the reversal is rather an uphill task.

Yet here are some ideas that are known to help:
* Drink four tablespoons of lemon juice every day on an empty stomach. Continue this treatment for a week. It will help to eliminate the gallstones. Also drink plenty of water so that the process of flushing out the gallstones becomes easier.

* Combine the juice of cucumber, carrots and beets and drink twice daily.

* Pears are known to help in providing gallstone pain relief. Eating pears helps to soften the gallstones.

* Herbal extracts work well in treating gallstones. St. Johns Wort is a popular herb which you can prepare into a tea. Drink a cup of the tea several times daily. To make the tea, add a cup of boiling water to four or five leaves.

* Drink apple juice for a couple of days and then consume about three ounces of fresh lemon juice and three ounces of olive oil. You should be able to pass the stones with the help of this treatment.

* Citrus fruits contain pectin which is helpful in treating the problem of gallstones.

" Caffeine is known to prevent gallstones from forming. Two to three cups of coffee a day may help to reduce the risk of gallstones.

" Dietary fiber helps to regulate metabolism and aids in the removal of cholesterol from the body. Consume high fiber cereals or while grain breads

126) FRESH Slow ground wheat - the life-giver vs stale flour.

High speed grinding heats up the flour to such a high temperature that it is partially cooked in the grinding. The flour loses its nutritive properties and as it is precooked it starts rotting in storage. This flour is stale and stale food cannot give health.
High speed grinding denatures the wheat.
Slow-ground wheat will bring back all the health giving properties of wheat back into play by eating foods made with whole wheat flour that contains the germ and the bran as well as the endosperm, you are aiding your body's defenses
Solution:
- Go back to slow grinding to eliminate heating of wheat when being ground.
- Mechanise the old hand-operated grinding system process and thereby make it less fatigue-intensive.
- Generate employment for the non-educated work force by semi mechanizing it all.
- Nutritionally, by keeping all the vitamins and roughage intact, promote better health.
- Industrial high speed grinding has a Direct relationship with diabetes

and heart problems as Vit E along with other elements although in lesser quantity is destroyed and roughage becomes too fine to be effective.

Every consumer of wheat who is health conscious is our client. Every connoisseur of good taste will recognize the difference.

This slow ground wheat will bring back the taste and health factors that are still remembered. It is like other food products that have gone out of fashion but are remembered and always find a ready market like Buttermilk and fresh white butter, fresh loaf of bread. People are no fools. When it comes to health they understand the pros and cons very speedily.

<u>Dr PK's Holistic Medico Advisory</u> shared <u>Artbook's</u><u>photo</u>.

Mud, Mud baths, play in mud and Beauty treatments.
One of the best ways to immunise children against all the irritating
sicknesses that befall humans is to let them play with earth, mud, and
play barefoot. Let them stop in puddles and get dirty and wet.
Just make sure it does not go to any excess. All this play also helps their
mental acuities to develop properly.
This anti-bacterial "thinking" of modern life is taking the concept of
cleanliness too far. We forget our link to Mother Earth only at our peril.
We are born of it and to it we return.
This fellow is taking his work rather seriously!

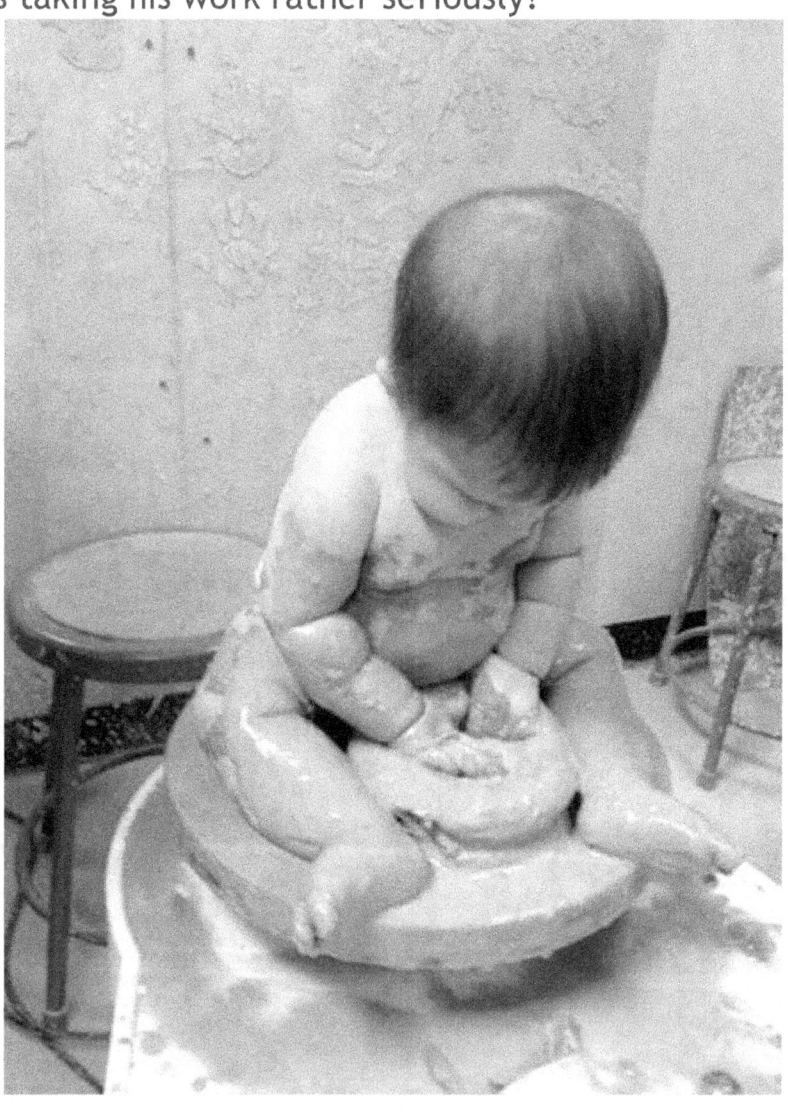

128) How can this dead food keep us alive and well?

Agreed; today medical technology has freed us from the fear of dying early. Agreed; that we do not fear any more big names like Typhus, Small pox, Tuberculosis, Whooping cough and many others.

But the argument remains that we are not as strong constitutionally as were our fore-fathers.

Agreed; we now live longer but I am not sure if we do not creak and groan more.

In the act of fighting off these illnesses we have weakened our own capacity to push back the onslaught of other debilitating illnesses that now come to us in more ferocious forms. We now need the crutches of special formulations to stave-off the attacks.

I am quite convinced that even this weakness is man-made and has roots in the way we process our food ingredients.

Specially, wheat, cooking oils and sugar. In the last century these items have been interfered with to an horrible extent, that although they retain the original name, yet by the time the processing has been completed – they are denatured, chemically altered and half-dead – often laced with poisonous materials too.

It would be a good idea to read up on the processing of these and you will realize how much they have been tampered with.

And the same can be said today of the entire food industry. How can this dead food keep us alive and well?

129) Dr PK's Holistic Medico Advisory shared a note.

Heat as an element in the industrial processes kills the natural nutrients in all foods. Watch-out!
Liquid poison masked as food?

As far as possible use rurally extracted oils, unrefined.
The best sources are olive, sesame, mustard, coconut and peanuts. Even better, use butter and butter-oil in minimum quantities, preferably extracted/made at home or a mom-pop owned dairy.

For rural communities and the urban poor, unrefined vegetable oils contribute significantly to the total amount of oil consumed. Crude oils are affordable to low-income groups and serve as important sources of b-carotene and tocopherols.
The industrially processed cooking oils that we buy in the market are lifeless refined greases.
Stripped, Garroted and Burnt at the stake - This is what they do industrially to the seeds they extract cooking oils from. They are neither healthy and at the same time all things enveloped in them also become non-digestible (non-processable by the body).

{Then where is all the oil that we are consuming going to and if the food is not being digested, what is happening to it?} - More on Industrial processing technique below.

COOKING OILS: Which oil to use?
08/01/2013 By Rebecca Leave
There are so many different types of cooking oils to choose from that it's sometimes difficult to determine which one to use. Below are some general tips and guidelines to help you determine which choice would work best for you and your cooking!

Some key things to remember when using different oils is to think about their smoke point:

High:Searing, deep-frying, browning, and all-purpose cooking

Medium:Baking, oven cooking, crisp or light sauté, stir-frying

Low:Low-heat baking and sauces or dressings

SesameOil:
■Smoke Point: Medium
■Has a rich, nutty flavor; high in antioxidants, Vitamins E & K
■Great for making sauces or dressings or for Asian dishes
■Store in the refrigerator

Flaxseed Oil:
■Smoke Point: No Heat
■Source of polyunsaturated fatty acids which aid in decreasing inflammation
■Best to use in things like dressings, heating it destroys beneficial omega-3s.

Olive Oil:
■Smoke Point: Low-Medium
■Heart healthy and high in antioxidants
■Use in low-heat cooking,baking, and dressings

Coconut Oil:
■Smoke Point: Medium
■Resists to oxidation very well, does not become rancid
■Contains lauric acid, which is shown to help improve the immune system
■Great for light fair and subtle flavor dishes

Peanut Oil:

- Smoke Point: Medium-High
- High in monounsaturated fats & vitamin E
- Has alight nutty flavor and a high smoke point which makes it great for deep-frying

Grapeseed Oil:
- Smoke Point: Medium-High
- High in vitamin E and polyunsaturated fats or omega 6
- Has a neutral taste; great for salad dressings
- Ideal for use as a cooking oil due to high smoke point: use for sautéing or stir-frying

Industrial Processing. Oil seeds are generally cleaned of foreign matter before dehulling.The kernels are ground to reduce size and cooked with steam, and the oil is extracted in a screw or hydraulic press. The pressed cake is flaked for later extraction of residual fat with solvents such as "food grade" hexane.Oil can be directly extracted with solvent from products which are low in oil content, that is, soybean, rice bran and corn germ.

Oil Refining.Refining produces an edible oil with characteristics that consumers desire such as bland flavour and odour, clear appearance, light colour, stability to oxidation and suitability for frying. Two main refining routes are alkaline refining (with chemicals) and physical refining (steam stripping, distillative neutralisation).

During deodorisation or physical refining, volatile components are removed from the oil by the combination of high temperature(180-220°C)., low pressure and stripping action of inert gas (steam). The degree of removal depends on the physical properties of the components (especially vapour pressure) and on the temperature and volume of steam passed through the oil. Some physical losses are highly desirable, for example, the removal of off-flavours, pesticides and polycyclic aromatic hydrocarbons, if present. Other losses of nutritionally valuable components, such as tocopherols and sterols, are potentially undesirable.

The above has been taken from:
http://www.fao.org/docrep/v4700e/v4700e0a.htm

130) Gluttony.

This is a kind of mind over matter disease. We eat because we love it; forgetting that food is primarily to feed the body so that this body can carry us through this life-time. If the food can be made tasty too and convenient that is a plus point.

But as understanding of laws of physics, chemistry and biology increased so did our temptations. Now we eat or pleasure. Even when we are eating well and good nutritious food we normally choose some selected dishes in exclusivity. This limits the variety of foods that we intake and often creates shortages of certain elements when continued over a long period of time. The deficiencies than culminate into illness.

Obesity and its attendant complications are now know to all and that is a direct manifestation of overeating for pleasure.

To be happy not much is required. But then our desires never stop sprouting.

If only we would focus more on the wishes that have been fulfilled and aspire for more but without agitation.

131) <u>Dr PK's Holistic Medico Advisory</u>
There are so many delightful healthy and nutritious things to titillate our taste buds!
Strawberry Delight (From Yahoo): Fresh strawberries wrapped in a sweet coottage cheese based 'cream', sinful on the lips, not the hips!

Ingredients: 2 litres toned milk, juice of 2 lemons, 6 tbsp powdered sugar, 12 medium strawberries

Method: Bring 2 litres of milk to a boil, turn off heat and add lemon juice. Stir until it curdles. Cover for 2 minutes. Strain through a muslin cloth, making sure all the liquid is drained. Remove this paneer from the cloth and churn in a blender for 3 seconds. Transfer to a flat plate and add powdered sugar. Mash by hand until a soft dough is formed and sugar is completely incorporated. Deep freeze for 20 minutes. Divide the mixture into 12 equal parts. Wrap each part around one strawberry. Refrigerate for 30-40 minutes. Slice each piece with a buttered knife. Serve chilled.

132) Dr PK's Holistic Medico Advisory shared Dr. Josh Axe'sphoto.
16 hours ago

When it comes to Holy Basil, we Indians believe in it so highly, that in every Hindu home it is prayed to as Mother Tulsa. It has special properties to help cleanse and repair the system. One of its active components was found to cure tuberculosis.

I take it first thing in the morning with water on waking up. It has helped me ward of allergic reactions that gave me breathing problems and small skin inflammations, warts and spots fell off and disappeared.

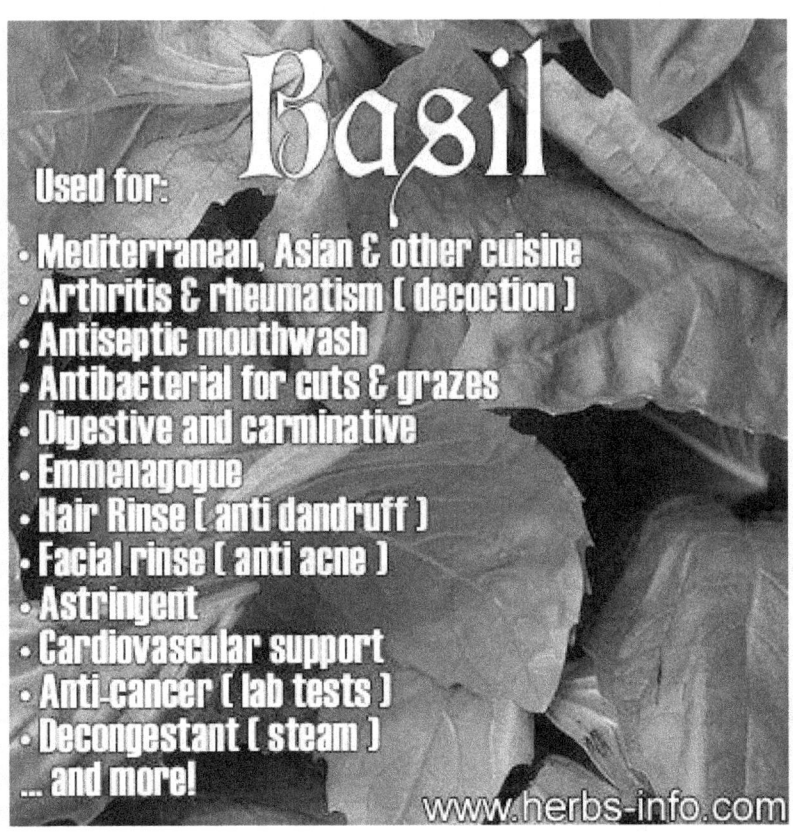

133) <u>Dr PK's Holistic Medico Advisory</u> shared <u>**Dead Fred's Genealogy Photo Archive**</u>'s <u>photo</u>.

One of the best ways to good health is by reining in the mind's incessant agitation and this is best done by promoting the reading habit.

The very act of sitting down to read is half way to achieve stillness and then focusing on the book makes it doubly more effective and of course if the book transposes you to another realm, then it has done its job.

Walking Library - London England c1940 . Books to Let , 6 pence /week .

(vsw tumblr)

134) Dr PK's Holistic Medico Advisory shared Dr. Josh Axe'sphoto.

People with migraine headaches may have lower levels of serum magnesium which affects serotonin receptors. Serotonin regulates pain messages in the brain. I recommend finding a high quality brand that does not contain magnesium stearate. However, the best way to boost your magnesium is through real foods like beans, dark leafy veggies, and seafood like wild caught salmon.
http://www.draxe.com/how-to-cure-your-headaches-all-naturally/

135) Dr PK's Holistic Medico Advisory

This is what fast food does to you. And also the new fangled fast-cook/microwave foods. Denatured flours. Artificial dressings. Transfats. Overheated and burnt-out oils. Artificial flavorings and questionable processes.
I recently saw a website purporting to be advising on healthy breakfast recommending margarine. From when did synthetically made margarine or such products became accepted as healthy?

Misleading adverts by responsible companies promoting breakfast cereals so highly processed that it is simply unimaginable as healthy and other stuff like boxed fruits juices laden with sugar or corn syrup as healthy juices is in my opinion unethical and really forces us to use our intelligence to think beyond all the misleading info that is being dished out.

136) *Gadgetry vs Common sense*.

This knowledge of understanding the body's needs by the signals it is sending has now been totally overshadowed by dependence on gadgetry. I am not for it.

Medically the practitioners of modern medicine have totally abdicated their diagnosing prowess. If the "tests" don't show it, they are unable to work out anything for themselves. After thousands of years of medicine practice how can this be?

But all the modern processes/gadgetry that have helped have also shown excessive misuse and are hurting in a big way in other ways. They have become more a source of income than need for diagnostic assistance.

There is also an accepted fact that there is an extensive Medicalization of Ordinary Life.

There is also a matter of attitude. We in the Indian tradition mostly would rather depart and end this life when the time comes and saving lives is not so important in our way of thinking. Our way of thinking is either cure me or let me go.

Keeping people alive by all means fair and foul is not in our philosophy and that is how we see the western medicine doing things. We see people being amputated, cut and drugged in the name of treatment and this is not our way.

What people don't realise that I am a great fan of "technology" - Specially in healthcare.
There are many products I advise people to take because they can other wise not know what to do to obtain all the nutrients in the right form:
Horlicks - one of the oldest products going around is a first class drink for all occasions without burdening the system. I even use it in my coffee instead of milk to slow the absorption of sugar and the insulin response that sugar initiates.
Complan Protein milk-whey mix for children and convalescing people - easy to make and takes care of most needs in a simple affordable package.
Multivitamin supplements - helps everybody; simple to take and portable enough to never miss taking it.
Protinex- Hydrolyzed Protein for vegetarians and others who cannot afford otherwise.
(I am naming these brands as they are the ones I know and use and are available in India)

Most people get into the habit of eating only some given dishes that they like. This limits their nutrient intake to such an extent that most begin to suffer from some deficiency or the other which eventually translates into serious illnesses.
What I am against is the food-like products that are poisons in bright packaging that the industry is dishing out knowingly. This is really evil.

In the picture below, you will notice that the products in the Cancer Producing list are all heavily processed and there is a high use of technology.

We really need to learn to avoid convenience and taste as the guiding factor in our selections of food.

137) <u>Dr PK's Holistic Medico Advisory</u>

from Yahoo Lifestyle.
Kale - one of my personal favorites.
"If there's one veggie that every nutritionist across the country eats and recommends, it's kale. That's because the leafy green is so nutrient-dense. It's loaded with vitamins K, A, and C, fiber, and calcium. And it's packed with so many cancer-preventative antioxidants and anti-inflammatory nutrients. My favorite way to eat more is making kale chips, a total party favorite and kid pleaser. Just rip up the kale, massage a little olive oil into the leaves, and bake at 375°F for 10 to 15 minutes. They're as good as potato chips!" -Carolyn Brown

138) SUPPLY ALL THE ELEMENTS THE BODY NEEDS & THE BODY WILL MAKE ITS OWN MEDICINE TO CURE ITSELF. This is: Orthomolecular Therapy - also known as Megavitamin Therapy..

There are primarily 40 nutrients that the body takes in every day to produce over 10,000 compounds. Most of these nutrients come from the food we eat and the water and air that we take in unconsciously. The lack of even one element results in a few tens or even hundreds of compounds to go missing. A fully healthy body, going at full steam, will falter when it does not get all the nutrients it needs. When this lack continues for a long period of time, permanent damage can occur due to chemical imbalances that are bound to break the chain.

A completely well person is rare to find. Humans have never been very careful with the care of their bodies. The industrial development has only expanded the range of misuse. That things are not well is apparent. We manage to get along on the strength of highly potent medication and marvelous surgery is available to make in-situ repairs. The human race merrily bumbles along.

A little understanding and a little care are all that is required to keep well. Therefore we need to learn the basics of natural therapeutics. Natural therapeutics is nothing new. We need to regain the lost art of natural healing, backed by today's surer knowledge.

Now few million years have gone into the making of the present-day man and the human race as we see it today. Nature has been quietly at work to produce this efficient machine that we call the human body. The tragedy is that it is not fully understood how the details work, but at least the basics are known.

Even if we are eating well and living correctly, a point to note is that in the past few generations, the intake of food has gone down in quantity. We are exerting less, so we need less food. This is in turn reducing the intake of the nutrients. The positive side of our scientific breakthroughs have also given us the solutions in the form of supplements that are easy to take and very convenient indeed.

179

An old adage says: EAT ONLY THAT FOOD WHICH ROTS AND DO IT BEFORE IT DOES. Avoid foods that have been processed and preserved too long. Live in a way so that all the very minimum needs of the body for relaxation and exercises are met. There is a hefty increase in the needs of nutrients because the levels of stresses and strains have been exponentially augmented by our desire to have more and live comfortably. We must absolutely reduce irritants like noise and polluted areas, if we can. A little observation of the cycle of nature will give us the key.

Even if you reach a point where treatment becomes an absolute necessity, it has to be remembered that medication can only help you pass over the bump, but for the cure the strength and vitality needed has to be provided by the body. A good question to ask at this juncture would be as to where does the body gets its vitality. Without the life force, medication is useless.

Just two examples will open your eyes: the indiscriminate use of air conditioners, which robs the body of its flexibility to adjust to temperature and weather changes, and the excessive watching of television which is creating vitamins A & D deprived couch potatoes with poor eyesight, paunch bellies, high cholesterol levels, and absolutely no capacity to take even the slightest physical stress. This lifestyle robs the mind of its analytical prowess, overloads the emotions with negative thoughts, and increases the desires unending. This is the perfect formula to disaster and a one-way ticket to the psychiatrist's couch.

When the body is young, it can take much abuse. As it grows older, it gets tired and it is unable to repair itself even with assistance. So intelligence dictates in keeping the body well supplied with all nutrients right from younger days so as to protect it from the elements and damage.

Most of the multi-vitamin & mineral preparations available today contain the elements that we need to concern with. These are unfortunately in short supply in 99% of the people you may meet today; specially in the city culture. The products in the market are designed and dosages are regulated as supplements. In illness the body needs all of these in greater quantity. So if you feel that your body is weakening but not really sick, giving these over-the-counter multivitamins in 3-4 times the usual dose. This dosage can give the support the body needs to cure itself. It has to be followed by some correction in the eating and other habits.

It would be good idea to study this subject more in detail. Good books and lectures are available in plenty.

I give here the link to one such site to get you started: http://orthomolecular.org/index.shtml

139) EGGS.

I am a staunch believer in the nutritional value of eggs. And they are so easy to cook and use in other dishes. I love them.

Eggs

"You'll find a carton of eggs in any R.D.'s fridge, including mine. Eggs have gotten a bad rap due to their cholesterol content, but research shows there's limited evidence linking egg consumption and heart disease. Plus, this protein-rich food has 70 calories, 13 vitamins and minerals, and the anti-inflammatory nutrient choline, which most Americans need." -Jennifer McDaniel

thru Yahoo lifestyle.

140) Notice all the food that are heavily processed are the evil ones.

141)   What I have always been repeating. Pay attention to your body's signal. Sickness if dealt with rightly at the very first stage can be stopped right there in its tracks. I use homeopathy and natural therapeutics; it works.

I keep 2 mixtures always at home. 1- Arsenic Album+ Lycopodium+Silicea+Sulfur & 2 - Carbo Veg+Nux vom+ Ipecac + Chelidonium.

The first one takes care of allergies, minor pollution related infections, sniffles, colds, fevers even food related infections and helps to cleanse the blood stream and the colon specially. In long term use they can clear old diseases too.

The second is good for acidosis, liver related problems, traveling sickness, heart burn and indigestion.

At the first sign of discomfort/discovery of symptoms they should be administered.

There are of course other products too that are kept on our shelves at all time to take care of any emergency that may build up – the focus is that it should be dealt with without delay before it has had time to grow roots in the body.

We are ardent fans of Chyawanprash (tradionally made gooseberry jam) fortified with ashwagandh (Indian ginseng) and saffron – this is taken regularly to fight of damage by he daily environmental exposure and + I advice taking it as medicine in colds and fever by increasing the dose to 4 spoonfuls every hour or two with a little milk.

This is news to me and good.

Green Tea + Chilli Eliminate Early Stage Cancers in Humans: This could be a major breakthrough. Human volunteers that tested positive for very early stage cancers (according to the presence of ENOX2 proteins) were given a 350 mg pill of green tea extract + chille pepper extract (from guajillo, a mild pepper) to take 6 X daily. After 3-6 months, 94% of the subjects which had previously tested positive for ENOX2 cancer markers now showed no detectable ENOX2, implying that their very early stage cancers were no longer present.

142) Two conversations that should be heard by all.

Does cancer on the mind manifest cancer?

Dr PK: If it is on your mind, it is because something in your consciousness is putting 2 & 2 together and giving a warning. You are aware of certain facts and your body's warning signals are working together to make you take protective/defensive action. That you will take or not depends on how strongly your mind's other faculties are working and to what they give priority. Humans tend to give importance to things only when they have reached crisis levels. It would be prudent to listen what your instinctive intelligence is saying.

Any suggestions for brain tumor?

Dr PK's : If it has reached that level then it is somewhat late in the day but I would suggest you take this combination of homeopathic medicines: 1- Arsenic Album+Lycopodium+Silicea+Sulfur and live in a more natural way - avoid high tension electrical areas including at home if you have too many electrical products around you and/or cabling surrounding you, WiFi etc.

My spiritual Guru used to say Brain tumor is always connected to desire for money or/and envy for others being able to have it.

143) When all the accounts are done, this would be more valuable than the diamond. Yet I would never not accept a diamond in gift for it would buy me a million tomatoes.
Eloísa Díaz's photo

144) Vegetarian or otherwise? Does it matter?

I neither recommend meat eating nor decry it
In desert areas meat or anything rots fast and becomes poisonous so it was not in vogue + keeping livestock was difficult as there is no FEED.
I eat eggs but am basically vegetarian. Our families come from the desert and since hundreds of years meat has not been eaten in our Maheshwari community which is a very large one
We have developed a whole range of foods that last weeks easily and cooked with whatever is available

Acidity due to bad eating habits is bad and permits disease to take roots. This knowledge of Pitta and other constitutions has been the basis of Ayurveda and all traditional medicinal systems (anywhere in the world in tribal local medicine). This is how it was in the natural world. And if we can change our acidic habits, an immediate improvement is seen.
A little countering needs to be done to impress people that they cannot continue with their present life styles and habits and hope for improvement by adding a few odd and end stuff into their lives.
We are talking bare factual pragmatism to counter many assumptions created by general thinking and propagating by gossip of the finer kind that eating tomatoes/lettuce/broccoli people who are sick due to bad nutrition/habits will be cured.
Often when I meet people with low resistance and bad constituion I even recommend chicken soup. Eggs are very good source of certain elements, not found easily otherwise.
The philosophical angle:...............
The truth is that things will be done or NOT done because they are in tune or not in tune with our own flowering and development.
Eating habits are geographical, based on the food available in a particular region.

Genetically it is not advisable to change habits suddenly.
Then try to imagine in the time of Buddha, how things would have been without MEDICARE/ambulances, refrigeration or electricity as TODAY and SUPERMARKETS WITH FOOD FROM ALL OVER THE PLANET.

One ate to live and ate what was available. Meat was a rarity, mostly on festivities.

It is another matter that as you grow in consciousness and sensitivity to the Cosmos, your needs change and you change your habits too. Mostly, when you near Buddhahood, your appetite patterns change because you also learn to absorb and take in energy from the air directly. A little easy to digest food from the plant world are found to be more than enough.

This business of being vegan or celibate or hermit will directly raise consciousness is downright silly. Although I may admit that it can eventually create a predisposition.

145)   Why are we so ready to tolerate discomfort and pain?

Inflammation.

Humans of the 21st century are an inflamed lot. The entire internal body is suffering from inflammation. I believe this is mainly due to the toxins that the body is not able to eliminate properly. This is easily rectified with intermittent fasting.
There are now new chemical compounds in foods, water and air that have no business to be there. They irritate and infect from within; subverting the entire system. A body that is constipated, not sweating properly or not urinating effectively due to lack of adequate water intake are most likely to suffer the most.
But at the same time the inflammation does not go down in a day or so. This takes longer. For this we need to go on a bland diet for 6 weeks or so; steamed vegetables, yoghurt, sautéed stuff, oranges and lemons, banana and pineapples and such goodies. Simple in structure and minimal cooking and very very easy on the digestive process. The moment you start feeling full – stop. It is best to leave some empty space in the stomach for it to do its churning properly. (Think of your clothes washing machine – what will happen if you stuff the barrel too tightly?)

The feeling of relief, less pains due to less inflamed nerves and arteries resulting in better circulation and functioning of the system will transpose you to a feeling heavenly well-being.

Inflam Inflammation From Wikipedia,

mation (Latin, *īnflammō*, "I ignite, set alight") is part of the complex biological response of vascular tissues to harmful stimuli, such as pathogens, damaged cells, or irritants.

Progressive destruction of the tissue would compromise the survival of the organism. However, chronic inflammation can also lead to a host of diseases, such as hay fever, periodontitis, atherosclerosis, rheumatoid arthritis, and even cancer (e.g., gallbladder carcinoma). It is for that reason that inflammation is normally closely regulated by the body

146)   Please let them pass on:

A weak constitution cannot support anything. I have seen operations being performed on terminal cases in the hope by the family and patients that it will put hem back on track; often the doctors not giving the true picture for it is not their decision always. It is criminal. The operation only speeds up the race to death may prolong it for a while in great pain but in the final analysis only impoverishes the family and causes much pain to the sick.

Reminds me of Voltaire's quote where he talks of doctors who know little, pouring medicines that they know even less about in the human body of which they know nothing: Curing the disease and killing the patient.

Kay Sluterbeck:

We treat animals better than people. My veterinarian has told me several times that there was no use trying to do anything further to save a desperately ill or very old animal. If the animal is suffering we end his suffering – if it is very old, we let it go gently into that good night.

Why not for the humans too?

147)   Dr PK's Holistic Medico Advisory

Life Force.

The body wants habits and the straight and narrow path of undisturbed equilibrium. The mind needs the opposite to grow and expand.

Keep to the middle path and tap into the Chi or as the French say, you shall be "boulversé".

Chi is the life force that flows in nature. It is akin to circulation of air in a dwelling. Where there are no windows, there is darkness and suffocation. Similarly when the body remains in a stationary position, consumes only limited produce in exclusivity, lives a life with limited motivation and ideas (more often than not - prejudices) a small hard-core, mothballed individual begins to evolve.

Tai Chi breaks this block harmlessly and with little yet pleasurable effort. All one needs to do is to take time out to go into Mother Nature's lap for a while. Try to stop talking and listen to one's inner being or at least just be silent outwardly. At the same time with eyes half closed, begin to concentrate on the your body and start moving your arms and torso, hands, feet, legs and head in a flowing motion that is circular, non-ending.

Keep all the joints a little bend so that there is no indication of rigidity. And go on and on; slowly and without jerks; One movement effortlessly merging into another. With your body trying to merge into all the possible sources of Chi that may be coming from the earth, plants, trees, air and from all the directions…….. Imagining yourself in the center of a swirling flow of Chi and you tapping into it.

Chinese who were and still are very close to the movement of the Chi, knew everything about it and the art of Tai Chi, Acupuncture and Feng Shui developed from this insight.

148) FEVER.

Fever is an essential part of the healing process. It is not a good idea to suppress it with Paracetamol simply because you don't like it. The infectious organisms are designed to be killed by the higher temperature. So, if, for any reason like getting a chill, you have fever let it be. If the fever goes to dangerous levels then a small dose of Paracetamol is definitely ok.

My personal way is to take half a tablet then and the other half 4 hours later. So that it becomes comfortable but the temperature still remains a little high so that the pathogens do not get the opportunity to start multiplying/proliferate again.

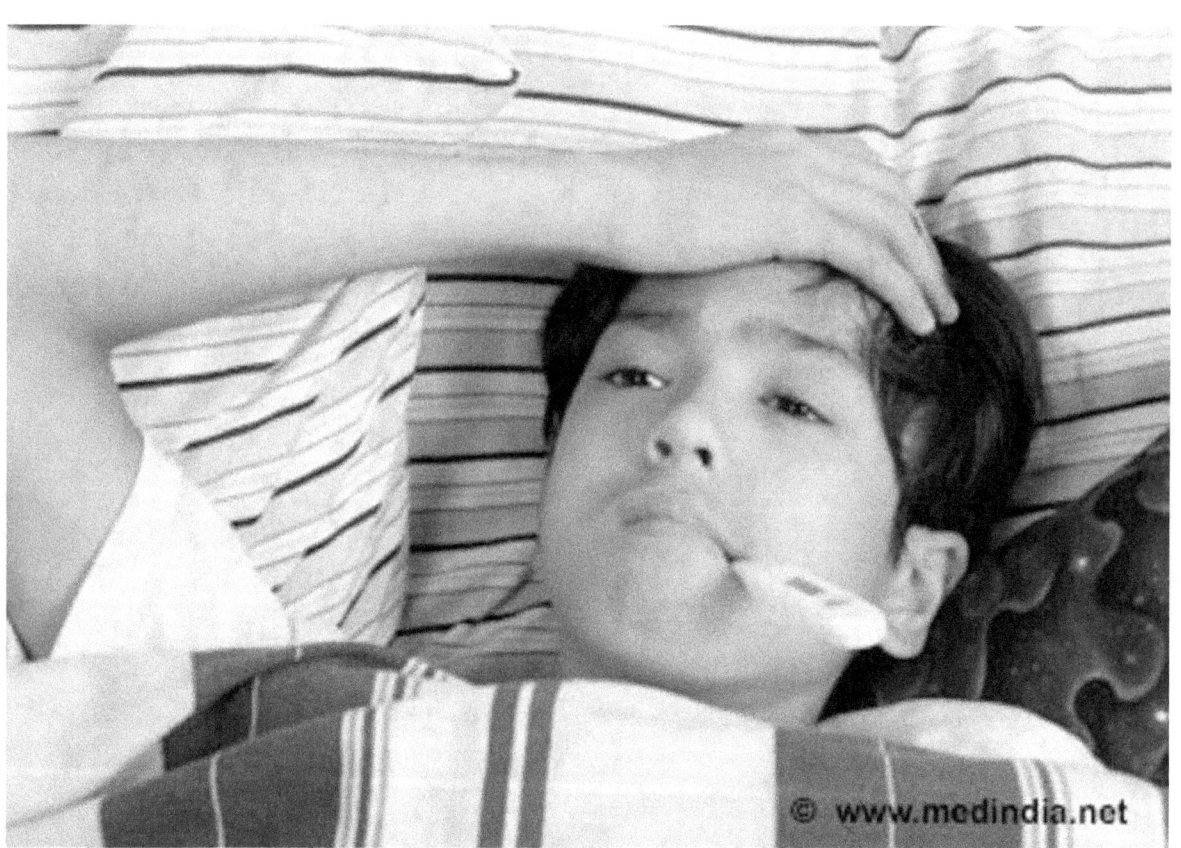

© www.medindia.net

148)   I am totally against the excessive and generalised routine use of MRIs, CT Scans and X-rays and other high radiation diagnostics.

There is a dramatic increase in the rates of thyroid cancer. Chief among these factors is the increased exposure we all have to different forms of radiation (nuclear accidents, greater use of CAT scans and other high radiation diagnostic tests, jet travel, etc.). Some experts like Davidson believe that the increased use of CAT scans in the past 20 years directly parallels the increasing incidence of thyroid cancers during the same period of time.

Who is to say that when the thyroid is affected, the other parts are left untouched?

We ignore all these signs and accept the claims that the dosages are safe; perhaps "yes" in isolation but is it all happening in isolation? Besides radiation we now have microwaves too.

The doctors have started advising routine precautionary check up using scans all. I totally disagree to this philosophy.

149) The Body is NOT a dumping ground.

If some is good more is not better. Satisfaction and comfort from food I can understand but binging I cannot. After-all the discomfort that ensues in the short run and the illnesses in the long run are all ours. Then most of the stuff people gorge-on is contra-indicated for the well being of the body
Learn from the wine tasters. They don't drink the wines they are tasting. They enjoy the taste and spit out. They drink when they sit down to drink for real. You are alive. You will be here for some time more. Relish your food and leave the rest for next time.

You can't fix your health until you fix your diet.

150) There is a remarkable tendency to first ignore symptoms and later to look for some single ingredient that will act as cure-all. I notice people like to think that if they focus singularly on a product to cure their ailments, like magic bullets, everything will soon get alright. This is an error.

Balanced food, foods that help in maintaining chemistry balance and even correct imbalances before they go out of control is the route to good health. For instance take these herbs and other products; use them often in such a way that your body chemistry is always in balance and that the need to go for a cure never arises.

Healing Herbs and Spices:

7 Adaptogen Herbs to Lower Cortisol -->http://draxe.com/7-adaptogen-herbs-to-lower-cortisol/

151) Sore muscles are difficult to treat. Try this next time. I just love having ginger in lemon with food and a concentrated ginger tea.

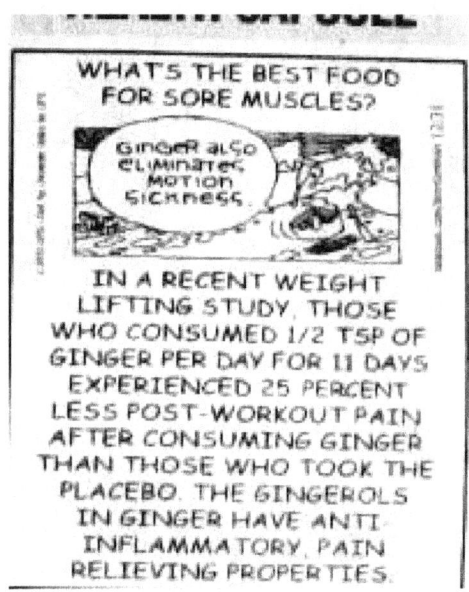

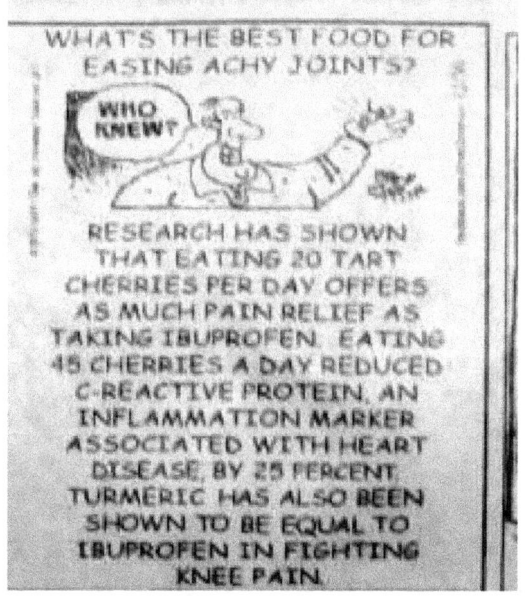

In India boiling a little turmeric with milk and drinking or pains and bruises and mild infections is quite the norm.

152) The magic of cloves.

Cloves Kill 91% of Breast Cancer Cells & Slow Growth by 78%: Eugenol, which is the major essential oil in cloves, was found to potently kill over 91% of three kinds of human breast cancer cells in vitro (MCF 10A, MCF7 and MDA-MB-231) which includes aggressive triple-negative breast cancer. This was done at a remarkably low dose of just 4 micromolar. When given to mice, the essential oil slowed breast tumor growth by a remarkable 78% over 28 days. Cloves are a powerful medicinal herb with established anti-inflammatory, antioxidant and anticancer properties. They have been used in Ayurvedic medicine in India for centuries, and recent studies are now confirming cloves' potent activity against prostate cancer, lung cancer, throat cancer, melanoma and others. India has one of the highest consumptions of herbs and spices in the world, and cloves are one of the major spices used in Indian cuisine. So it's not surprising that the rate of breast cancer there is just one quarter of that in

American or European women (IARC 2012 data). Cloves could therefore be a very healthy addition to a balanced diet focused on organic fruit and vegetables.
#Cancer #Cloves #BreastCancer
http://www.ncbi.nlm.nih.gov/pubmed/24330704

153) ENERGY SUPPLY

We in India believe that the Soul supplies the energy. To stupidly waste it on frivolities is so a sign of ignorance and lack of awareness. Let us show some wisdom in our use of energy and use it to be healthy and to create something for this world that will benefit all now and later. Where does all your energy come from? Why you are alive and why suddenly you are dead?

When you lose your temper, is it you in the rage or some other being using you to destroy things around you? Anyway again, where does this energy come from?

All the pleasures of the body that we enjoy like sex, whiskey & Bourbons, overeating just to enjoy the taste, adventures for excitement like bunging – extreme sports; where and who supplies the energy to make it all possible?

Sex is concentrated energy located somewhere in the persona that makes you. When you use it for pleasure you are enjoying a short moment of exalted status but depleting your store of energy in huge quantity. This something thrown out and it is so highly concentrated that the entire body and spirit is depleted for some time. Too often and it can weaken you to no end.

Similarly when drink and food are consumed in excess, more energy is used up in digesting and purifying the system later. That little moment of taste become a big burden on the body. Overweight/obesity is now a huge problem and the extra energy to just move around has to be coming from somewhere, isn't it? Do you never feel the blood being sucked out of you from all these indulgences and yet you dream of forever being young and able?

154) <u>Dr PK's Holistic Medico Advisory</u> shared <u>angemaya</u>'s <u>photo</u>.

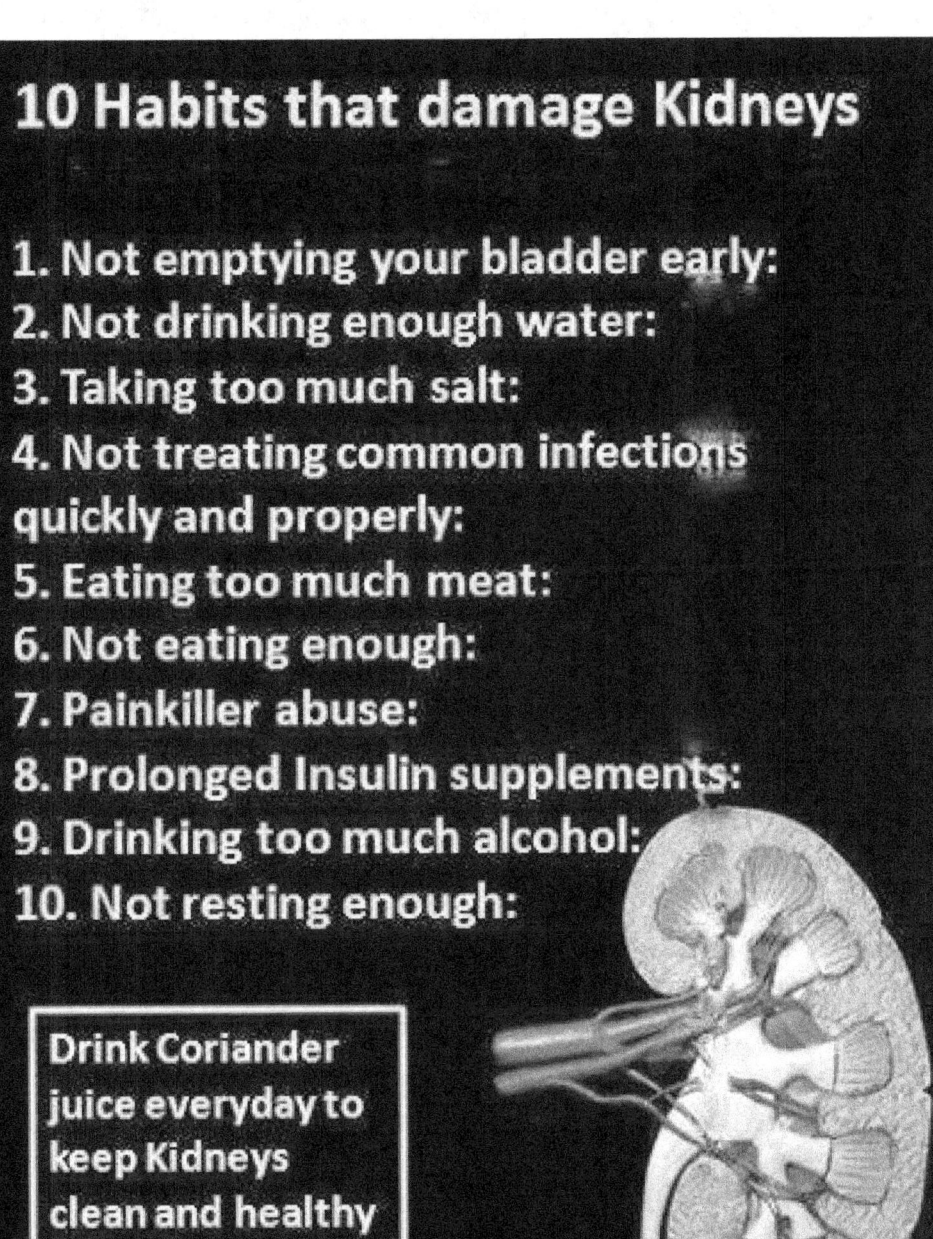

155)

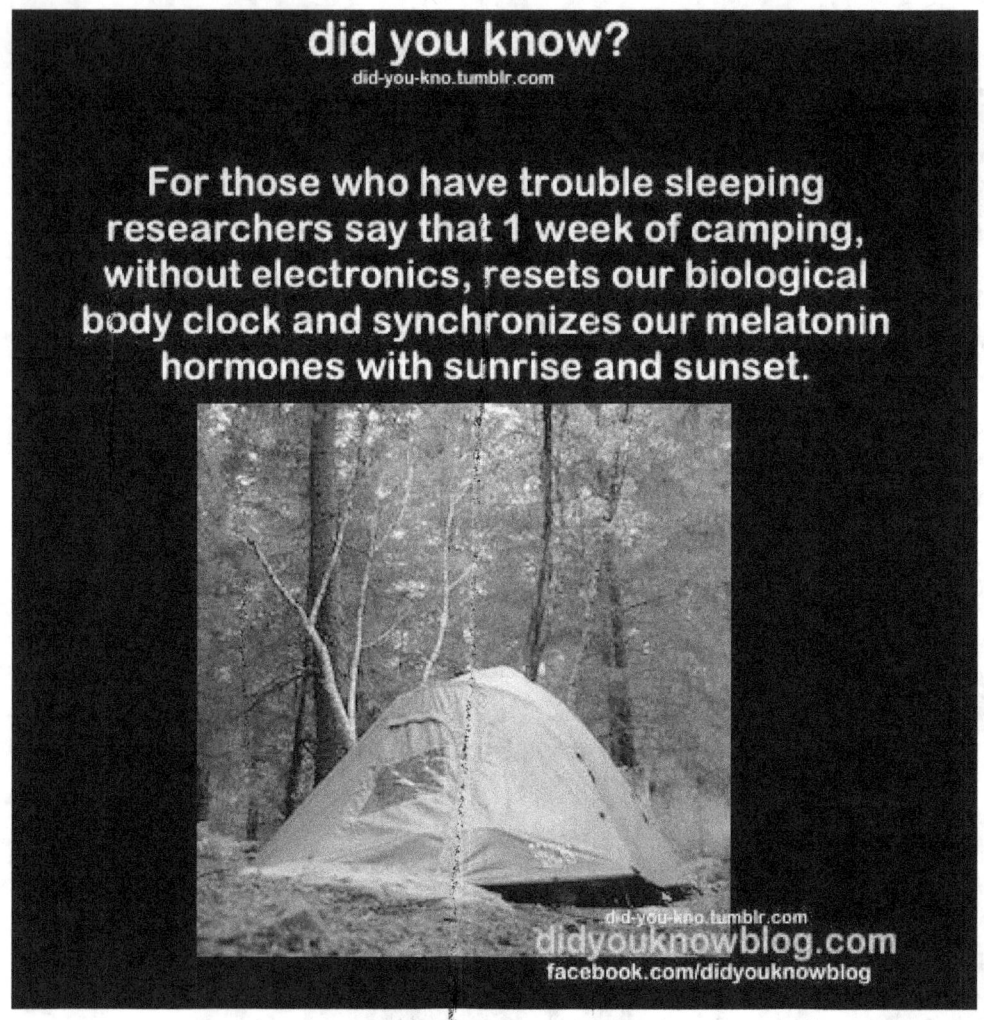

Additional information to understand yourself better

Rid Your Body of Toxins the Natural Way
Dr. Craig Sommers
Since 1997 I have been working with clients, testing them for toxic minerals and, if present, helping them to rid their bodies of toxic mineral accumulation. In my 17 years of practice while also studying the work of researchers in this field, I have learned that the body does not usually store toxic minerals found in food unless there is a deficit in the look alike nutritional mineral. Allow me to explain.

Many of the toxic minerals are similar in atomic size and electron configuration to specific nutritional minerals. When a human body is low in a particular essential nutritional mineral, it will look for another similar mineral to use in place of the nutritional mineral. Unfortunately, in many cases, the similar mineral is a toxic mineral.

Here is a list of nutritional minerals with the corresponding toxic minerals that have a similar configuration. To the body:

Selenium looks similar to mercury.

Zinc looks similar to cadmium.

Calcium looks similar to lead.

Magnesium looks similar to nickel, aluminium, and uranium. All three may accumulate if magnesium is deficient.

With arsenic, protective minerals include selenium and zinc. Sulfur containing amino acids also help the body reduce arsenic toxicity along with the vitamins B12 and folate.

The way that it works is quite simple. For example, if the body tests high in cadmium, it is very likely that the person is deficient in zinc. This usually happens because the person has not been consuming enough zinc on an ongoing basis to fulfill their body's needs. The person needs to up their zinc intake by consuming foods high zinc, such as pumpkin seeds, and a nutritional supplement with a human-useable form of zinc is also important. When the body finally gets the zinc that it needs, the cadmium will be excreted slowly over time and the body will not continue to store cadmium in the future.

This principle goes with food as well. For example, if you were able to get a complete mineral profile of a favorite food and found it had a high level of cadmium, you would also look at the level of zinc and want to see that the zinc level was quite a bit higher in that food than the cadmium level. In that scenario, the body would be more likely to absorb the zinc and discard the cadmium.

walnuts_picIt is also important to know that minerals are found in many forms. For example, zinc supplements can be found as: zinc oxide, zinc gluconate, zinc carbonate, ionic zinc, etc. Some forms such as zinc oxide are very poorly absorbed by the body while other forms such as ionic zinc are highly absorbable and usable by the body. The form of the mineral is key.

Toxic minerals also come in different forms. For example, the type of arsenic usually found in food, known as organic arsenic, has a much lower toxicity level than the nonorganic form of arsenic found in the earth. In fact, according to scientists, arsenic found in fish, known as arsenobetaine, is nearly non-toxic. [1] Please note that the form of mercury found in fish is quite dangerous and should be avoided.

In conclusion, practically all types of food have some level of toxic minerals in them. Humans and all other species on this planet have evolved with both, nutritional and toxic minerals. Our bodies are usually capable of eliminating the toxic minerals found in food, provided they have adequate amounts of the corresponding nutritional mineral. We just need to make sure that our bodies do not go into nutritional mineral deficit and try to use and store toxic minerals in place of the nutritional ones.

Craig B Sommers ND, CN

- See more at: http://www.sunwarrior.com/news/rid-body-toxins-natural-way/#sthash.Xe05YUFt.dpuf

CHICKEN SOUP
REALLY CAN HELP RELIEVE
COLDS AND FLU BY
AFFECTING THE WHITE
BLOOD CELLS THAT
CAUSE FLU SYMPTOMS.

«Jogging or running or even exercising heavily sends a message to your brain that the body needs MORE nutrients & food to sustain this kind of activity»

«It sounds weird to say, but it is much healthier to be a couch potato and indulge in eating fast-food then to be running 10 miles a day, and eating then trying to satisfy the false hunger pangs that can result in eating four times what your body really needs.

Exercise is way over rated and probably more hazardous to your health then a normal healthy sedentary lifestyle» claims the specialist.

Even if you ran a marathon every day, you wouldn't lose weight unless you consumed fewer calories than you burned. The bottom line to losing weight is burning more calories than you consume, no matter how much exercise you do.

Quercetin: a Powerful Natural Antihistamine
Quercetin is a Powerful Natural Antihistamine: Quercetin is a flavonoid with proven anti-allergic properties both in lab studies and on humans. It suppresses the release of histamines and also reduces inflammatory response. Quercetin is such a powerful antihistamine in fact, that in one study it actually suppressed the anaphylactic reaction to peanuts in allergic mice. In another study, it outperformed a commercially available drug in suppressing allergic contact dermatitis in humans. The best sources of dietary quercetin (which is a flavonoid) include spinach, cabbage, celery, peppers, onions, citrus fruit, apples, berries and Spanish red wine. If that's not enough, quercetin supplements are available on the market and there are many anecdotal reports that these help to reduce general allergy symptoms (to pollen, mold, dust). As side benefits, quercetin is also a potent antioxidant and anti-inflammatory, and may reduce the risk of heart disease and cancer. In lab studies, it has shown strong activity against melanoma, breast cancer, cervical cancer, prostate cancer, colon cancer and lung cancer. If you've got allergies, you may want to consider adding more quercetin-rich fruit and vegetables to your daily diet, or even taking a supplement. A link to the USDA's database on the quercetin content of foods is below.
#Quercetin #Allergy #Antihistamine
http://ars.usda.gov/Services/docs.htm?docid=6231

WHICH HERBS AND SPICES ARE MOST EFFECTIVE AT REDUCING PAIN AND INFLAMMATION?

The active ingredient of the turmeric plant is curcumin.

FOUR SPICES — CLOVES, ROSEMARY, GINGER AND TURMERIC — POSSESS THE MOST POWERFUL ANTI-INFLAMMATORY PROPERTIES OF ALL SPICES STUDIED. THESE SPICES PROVIDE RELIEF FROM PAIN AND INFLAMMATION WITHOUT THE SIDE EFFECTS OF DRUGS LIKE IBUPROFEN AND ASPIRIN.

The "Nightshade Vegetabes" are a food group implicated in both osteo-arthritis and rheumatoid arthritis.

What Are the Night-Shade Foods, and How Do They Cause Arthritis?

This is a group of plants including Tomatoes, Potatoes, Egglant, Peppers and Tobacco.

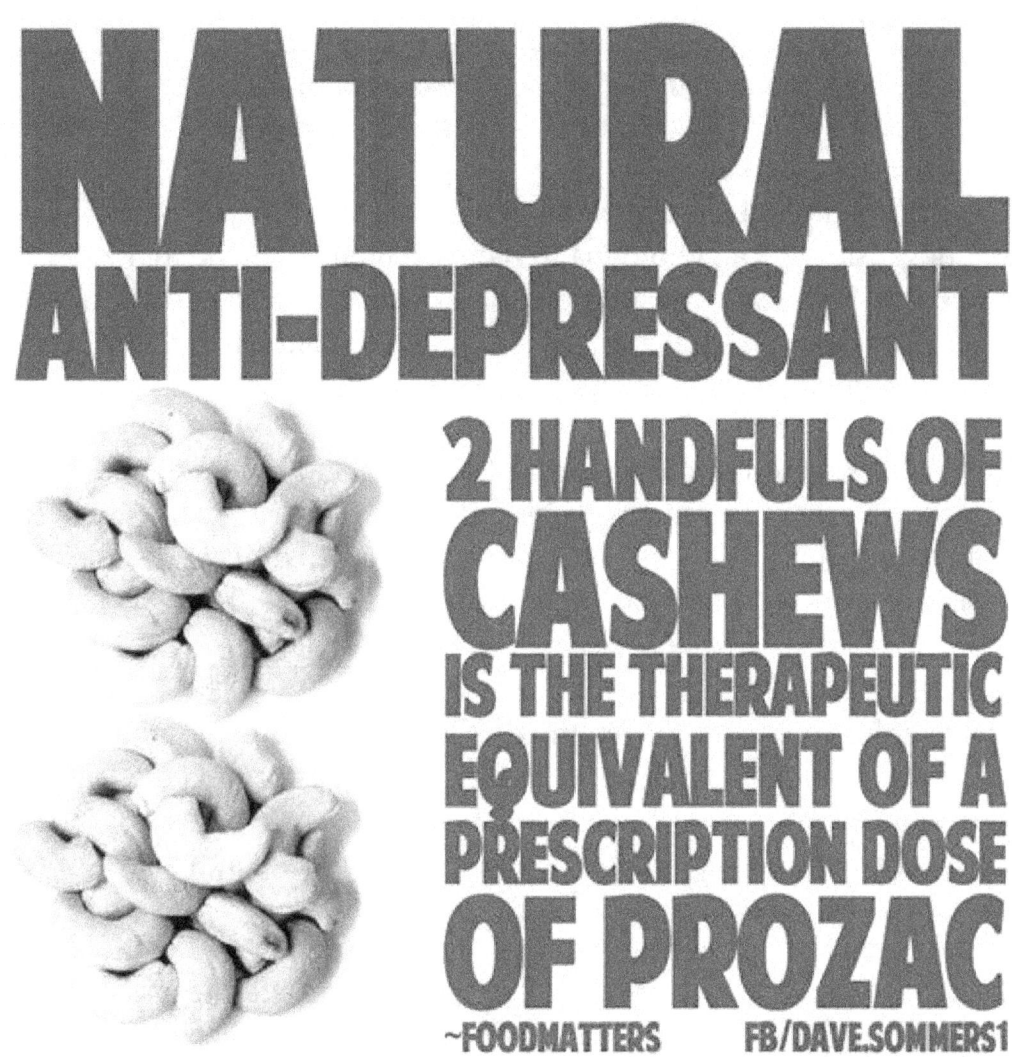

NATURAL ANTI-DEPRESSANT

2 HANDFULS OF CASHEWS IS THE THERAPEUTIC EQUIVALENT OF A PRESCRIPTION DOSE OF PROZAC

~FOODMATTERS   FB/DAVE.SOMMERS1

How packaged foods destroy your health

Canned foods: These foods have high quantities of preservatives like calcium, potassium and sodium salts and sodium benzoate that can cause serious health problems. Excessive intake of these foods could cause kidney, heart or liver damage.

Breads, cakes, cookies: Made from refined white flour instead of whole grains, most bakery products contain potassium bromate which is used to increase their volume. \"If the bread is not cooked long enough or not at a high enough temperature, then a residual amount of this oxidizing agent will remain in bread, which may be harmful if consumed,\" says Dr Nidhi Sarin, a clinical nutritionist.

205

Salty snacks and chips: These foods contain calcium, potassium and sodium salts that if consumed in excess can lead to high blood pressure, kidney damage, worsening of heart-related diseases, calcification of tissues and other complications.

Processed meats: According to Dr Sarin, sodium nitrate is used in processed meats such as ham, hot dogs, sausage and bologna to increase their shelf-life and maintain their colour. \"Excessive consumption of sodium nitrate is known to worsen asthma and decrease lung function. So one should avoid having packaged foods on regular basis and or at least check the amount of preservatives used before consuming them,\" she said.

Fruit juices, jams pickles: \"Sodium benzoate and benzoic acid are food preservatives found in sauces, fruit juices, jams and pickled products. If used over the permissible limit, regular intake can cause allergic reactions,\" said Ashok Kanchan, a researcher working with Consumer-Voice NGO.

Many people believe that the crux of a healthy diet is the exclusion of unhealthy foods. However, rather than just focusing on cutting things out, a good diet should also incorporate an increased intake of nutritious, health-boosting foods. Fortunately, there are many foods out there which will improve health and wellbeing as well as protect against future illness.

Nuts: Although nuts are high in calories and so should be eaten in moderation, the calories in nuts come mainly from their high levels of monounsaturated fats, which are extremely good for health. Eating foods rich in these fats can help reduce bad cholesterol and lower your risk of heart disease and stroke. As well as their heart benefits, nuts are also a great source of protein and are packed with fibre, antioxidants, fatty acids and vitamins and minerals. It is worth noting that peanuts are actually legumes and have different nutritional properties from tree nuts, but there are many other good options to pick from including Brazil nuts, cashews, walnuts, pecans and pistachios. L

Milk: Remember how your mother would force you to have 2 glasses of milk every day when you were a child? She would do it for a number of good reasons. Milk is extremely rich in calcium and also aids in burning fat. With increased cases of osteoporosis and arthritis among elderly males, a regular intake of fat-free milk will do wonders to their health. A glass of milk at breakfast, and one before going to bed will fulfil the daily dietary needs.

Eggs: Eggs are best sources of dietary protein. They are rich in choline and antioxidants which reduce the risks of breast cancer and eye diseases. Though most of us tend to abstain from eating eggs because of their cholesterol inducing properties, we fail to realise that consuming them in moderation will actually result in a healthy heart. Having an egg daily will boost the immune system and help the skin and hair glow with health. Heart patients, however, are advised to restrict their intake to two a week.

Dark, leafy greens: Dark, leafy greens such as spinach, watercress and kale are automatically associated with healthy eating for many due to the "eat your greens mantra" that has been drummed into our heads over the years. However, this faith in the health properties of green veg is well-founded, as these vegetables are bursting with nutrients including iron, calcium, potassium and vitamin C, and packed with health-boosting phytonutrients. Some of the reputed health benefits of eating your greens include lowered blood pressure, improved eye health and a reduced risk of cognitive decline.

Berries: Acai berry, blueberry, goji berry, blackberry... With a new "super berry" hitting the headlines seemingly every week, it can be hard to keep up with which berry you should be buying this week. Luckily, the truth of the matter is you generally can't go wrong with any commercially available berry. These super healthy fruits are extremely high in antioxidants and have many individual health benefits, including the ability to help prevent dementia (blackcurrants and boysenberries), fight off colon cancer (blueberries), improve vision (bilberries) and ward off urinary tract infections (cranberries).

Beans: From the macrobiotic to the student, many diets rely on the humble bean in its dry, tinned or baked form - and this could be great news for our health. Studies have found that beans are not only excellent weight-loss and energy foods, but they are a great source of antioxidants, protein and nutrients (such as iron, manganese and B vitamins). Beans are also an excellent source of soluble fibre, which can help to reduce cholesterol, stabilise blood sugar and improve the digestive system, while a study by scientists at the University College of London showed that beans can also help prevent cancer.

Tamarind pulp is commonly used in Asian cuisine and Worcestershire sauce due to its pleasing sour flavor. It aids constipation due to its laxative effect and is anti-helmintic, antibacterial and hypolipidemic. The fruit may promote eye health as it moistens cornea and researchers are investigating its chemical content similar to mucin that is known to wet the eye.

Some fruits like apple, banana, when cut turn brown on exposure to air. This unappealing browning can be avoided by coating the sliced fruit with a layer of sugar, salt or lime juice.

Fruits in rainbow colors synergistically boost immunity, revive and rejuvenate health and well-being.

Grapes have garnered attention due to its polyphenol - resveratrol that promotes longevity and several antioxidants shielding cardiovascular system. Grapes contain ellagic acid. Anthocyanins, found abundantly in red grapes and Catechins, a type of flavonoid found in green varieties also have health promoting effects. Grapes seeds also offer essential fatty acids and tocopherol.

---

l

Steamed Veggies-

Eating more vegetables is always a smart move, and steaming them could improve their cholesterol-lowering power even more. That's because steaming some produce, including asparagus, beets, okra, carrots, eggplant, green beans, and cauliflower, may help them do a better job of binding bile acids, which means your liver needs to use up more LDL cholesterol into order to make bile. That translates into less circulating LDL in your bloodstream.

Fish that are rich in omega-3 polyunsaturated fatty acids, like salmon, can directly lower you LDL count. It is recommended that you eat 2-3 servings of these fish a week, which can also help to lower your blood pressure and reduce your risk of developing blood clots.

I take oil capsules as I am a vegetarian by choice.

---

1. Cannabis works as medicine for anything that has a spine. Because anything with a spine has the endocannabinoid system.

2. The endocannabinoid system directly regulates the function of the immune system. When your immune system works right, it usually knows what to do.

3. Cannabis is not toxic. That means you virtually cannot lethally overdose the patient with this medicine. Nice, isn't it?

4. It works, it is cheap to produce. It is safe, harmless and effective.

Taking babies out in open traffic is bad for their development.
We cannot forget that they are just started to grow up and the growth can get stunted by pollution, bad food, extreme exposures to dust, noise, medicines like antibiotics and bad attitudes like lack of cuddling
Nitrogen dioxide comes from sources such as power plants and car exhausts, and this type of air pollution is associated with asthma and heart disease, the researchers said.
Of course the areas that are heavily polluted are also most population dense and are avoided by the rich so the poorest find it economical to stay there and so are the most exposed.

Spiritual depression presents itself in much the same way as clinical depression - but not quite. The marks of distinction are crucial, yet hard for the untrained to recognize. They make the difference between interpreting the source of depression as a problem that may require medication or as a process of transformation that is best served by reflection, discussion of the stages of the dark night, and understanding the nature of mystical prayer. I have met many people who have been treated for depression and other conditions when they were in fact, in the deep stages of a spiritual crisis. Without the proper support, that crisis becomes misdirected into a a problem with relationships, a problem with one's childhood, or a chronic malaise. Spiritual crises are now a very real part of our spectrum of health challenges and we need to acknowledge them with the same authority as we do clinical depression.

The 'heavy breakfast'
While some completely skip breakfast, there are others who take the "healthy breakfast" too seriously! It is true that breakfast provides energy to the body, and kick starts metabolism for the rest of the day. However, with this view, having calorie-laden foods in the morning is not a very wise idea. Simple carbohydrate-rich foods, like cakes, rice, pasta, white bread, and desserts and fried foods tend to make you feel lethargic throughout the day, apart from aiding weight gain. Try and incorporate as many fresh fruits, vegetables and whole grains in your breakfast, as possible.

IS COFFEE GOOD OR BAD FOR YOU?

COFFEE DRINKERS HAVE A 67 PERCENT LOWER RISK OF TYPE 2 DIABETES, A MUCH LOWER RISK OF PARKINSON'S DISEASE AND ALZHEIMER'S DISEASE, AND AN 80 PERCENT LOWER RISK OF LIVER DISEASE. STUDIES HAVE SHOWN THAT CAFFEINE CAN IMPROVE MEMORY, MOOD, REACTION TIME AND OVERALL BRAIN FUNCTION.

CAN DRINKING COFFEE LOWER MY RISK OF DIABETES?

MORE AND MORE STUDIES ARE POINTING TO THE HEALTH BENEFITS DERIVED FROM DRINKING COFFEE. AMONG THEM IS A 37 PERCENT DECREASE IN DIABETES RISK FOR THOSE WHO DRINK 24 OR MORE OUNCES OF COFFEE PER DAY. SUGGESTED AMOUNT FOR MAXIMUM BENEFIT: 3 TO 5 CUPS PER DAY.

Metals and the Mind
Posted on April 15, 2009 by Theresa Vernon •
The one thing we can say about the effect of toxic metals on the mind is that we don't know much. These metals are hard to detect and difficult to get rid of once you know you have them. That is why you don't hear much about this subject. I certainly didn't, even after studying nutrition, herbs and all kinds of natural therapies for years and years. You often hear, "Well, you could have heavy metal toxicity," but what does that mean? What do you do about it? All I had ever heard about for heavy metal toxicity was chelation and I didn't like what I heard.

The key fact about the metal toxicity is that it is always related to chronic fatigue and chronic adrenal fatigue.

Adrenal Fatigue

All chronic illness includes chronic fatigue and adrenal fatigue, whether you feel tired or not. A lot of my patients will say, "Oh, I have lots of energy," but they do not or they would not be chronically ill. There is no conventional medical treatment for adrenal fatigue unless you have reached the point of total failure, at which time you are put on cortical supplements for the rest of your life. Therefore, like the issue of toxic metals, if adrenal fatigue is not tested for, it is not discussed.

These two problems—adrenal fatigue and toxic metal buildup—are strongly related because you cannot excrete metal without good adrenal function. Adrenal function needs to be pretty close to normal or you will start retaining metals, because the adrenal glands have such a big part to play in the proper handling of metals in the body.

Adrenal Fatigue

WHAT YOU NEED TO KNOW
The adrenal glands are your body's primary "shock absorbers." These two little thumb-sized glands sitting on top of your kidneys produce hormones including norepinephrine, cortisol and DHEA that allow you to respond to the conditions of your daily life in healthy and flexible ways.
Norepinephrine (also called adrenaline) is commonly thought of as the fight-or-flight hormone. It's produced when something is (or you think it is) threatening.

This hormone makes your heart pound, your blood rush to your heart and large muscle groups, your pupils widen, your brain sharpen, and your tolerance for pain increase—basically, it prepares you for battle. Modern-day battles are most likely things like pushing your body to keep going when it's fatigued, dealing with a stressful job, and reacting with quick reflexes to avoid a traffic accident. Think of these adrenaline surges as withdrawals from a bank, to help you get through life's rough spots. If you have gotten into the habit of withdrawing adrenaline from your account too often, you'll eventually be overdrawn and your adrenal glands will be overwhelmed. Then, you'll have too little adrenaline when you really need it. Cortisol increases your appetite and energy level while toning down your immune system's allergic and inflammatory responses. This hormone stimulates the storage and release of energy in the body, helps the body resist the stressful effects of infections, trauma, and temperature extremes, and helps you maintain stable emotions. Synthetic versions of cortisol—prednisone and cortisone, for example— are often prescribed to help people perk up and feel better so they will eat, drink, and move around more and therefore be better able to fight off illness or heal from an injury. Ideally, cortisol is released into the system only on an occasional basis, rather than in response to chronic stress. If cortisol levels become too high for too long, they may have undesirable side effects, including loss of bone density, muscle wasting, thinning of the skin, decreased ability to build protein, kidney damage, fluid retention, spiking blood sugar levels, weight gain, and increased vulnerability to bacteria, viruses, fungi, yeasts, allergies, parasites, and even cancer.

Dehydroepiandrosterone (DHEA) is an androgen that is produced by both the adrenal glands and the ovaries. DHEA helps to neutralize cortisol's immune-suppressant effect, thereby improving resistance to disease. (Cortisol and DHEA are inversely proportional to each other. When one is up, the other goes down.) DHEA also helps to protect and increase bone density, guards cardiovascular health by keeping "bad" cholesterol (LDL) levels under control, provides vitality and energy, sharpens the mind, and helps maintain normal sleep patterns. Like norepinephrine and cortisol, DHEA also improves your ability to recover from episodes of stress and trauma, overwork, temperature extremes, etc. And if a woman is experiencing a decline in libido due to falling testosterone levels, often it is declining DHEA levels that are at the root of the testosterone deficiency, as DHEA is the main ingredient the body uses to manufacture testosterone.

If the intensity and frequency of the stresses in your life—either those internally driven (such as your perceptions about your life) or those externally driven (such as having surgery or working the night shift)—become too great, then over time your adrenal glands will begin to become exhausted. This will mean that you are much more likely to suffer from fatigue and menopausal symptoms. And a woman in a state of adrenal exhaustion is likely to find herself at a distinct disadvantage when entering perimenopause, because perimenopause itself is an additional form of stress.

Adrenal exhaustion usually suggests that there are long-standing life problems in need of resolution. These issues will loom all the larger when seen with the no-nonsense mental clarity of perimenopause, but not only will adrenal exhaustion make the transition needlessly unpleasant, it also can deprive a woman of the resources she needs to address those issues and to take full advantage of the creative promise of the second half of her life.

Abnormal adrenaline and cortisol levels can result in mood disorders, sleep disturbances, reduced resistance to disease, and changes in vital circulation. Because these side effects are not uncomfortable enough to be intolerable, a self-destructive, adrenal-depleting lifestyle often continues. DHEA, which helps the body recover from this sort of chronic abuse, gets revved up full time instead of only episodically. Gradually the adrenal glands become seriously exhausted, with the first and most profound effect being their waning ability to produce DHEA. As levels of this restorative hormone fall, cortisol and adrenaline levels begin to fluctuate as well, as the adrenal glands attempt to fill increasingly impossible orders for more support.

The result is often relentless, debilitating fatigue that is the hallmark of adrenal exhaustion. Though this fatigue is often accompanied by depressed mood, irritability, and loss of interest in life, this doesn't mean that the adrenal problem is necessarily the cause of the mood change, any more than similar problems are always caused by thyroid malfunction. That is why these emotional symptoms do not always go away with treatment—the underlying issues remain unresolved until they are specifically addressed by behavior and lifestyle changes.

LISTEN TO YOUR BODY

Here are some typical signs that your adrenals may need attention: You awaken feeling groggy and have difficulty dragging yourself out of bed. You can't get going without that first cup or two of caffeinated coffee or tea. You not only rely on sugary snacks and caffeine to get through the day but find you actually crave sweets, particularly in the late morning or afternoon. (Perhaps you've even been diagnosed with hypoglycemia.) Your thinking is foggy and you have memory problems. You suffer from recurrent infections, headaches and depression. At night, though exhausted, you have trouble falling asleep as the worries of the day replay in your head and you suffer from insomnia. Ordinary stresses have an impact that is out of proportion to their importance. You wonder what happened to your interest in sex. If this description fits you, your adrenals may be running on empty, even if all your conventional medical tests are normal.

Conventional blood tests, taken at whatever time your doctor has scheduled your appointment, might indicate that your adrenals are normal. However, a better diagnostic approach will test your levels at different times of the day, which is much more likely to reveal an out-of-whack pattern of cortisol or DHEA secretion. Adrenal fatigue is characterized by cortisol levels that are too high at night and not high enough in the morning.

WHAT CAUSES THIS

Unabated stress over long periods of time that is not addressed combined with a nutrient-poor diet is what usually leads to adrenal exhaustion.

HEALING ALTERNATIVES

If an adrenal test shows that you are producing inadequate levels of adrenal hormones, several routes are available for increasing either DHEA, cortisol, or both. First, you can take the hormone directly. If you take DHEA, opt for small doses of pharmaceutical grade DHEA (5–10 mg/day, but possibly up to 25 mg once or twice a day).[1] Have your levels retested every three months, and when levels return to the normal range, the dose should be gradually tapered until you're off the hormone completely.

Some individuals require very small doses of hydrocortisone, which can be used safely and effectively if prescribed by a health care provider knowledgeable about how and when to use it.

Be aware that if you supplement your adrenal hormones in dosages that are too high, or if you take supplements for too long, the result can be permanent depression of adrenal function.

SPIRITUAL AND HOLISTIC OPTIONS

A far better option over the long run is to restore adrenal health and function so your adrenals can eventually produce the hormones you need on their own. That will require making changes in the lifestyle that caused the adrenal depletion. Here are some suggestions:

Focus more on loving thoughts. Thoughts that bring you pleasure (like thinking about people you love, favorite pets, a delicious meal, or even a sweet memory) short-circuit the harm done by the body's physiological reaction to stress. This learning to "think with your heart" may be challenging at first, but it's definitely worth it. If you faithfully learn this and regularly pay attention to areas of your life that bring you joy and fulfillment, you will evoke biochemical changes in your body over time that will recharge your adrenal batteries. (For assistance, I recommend the training programs and books from The Institute of HeartMath.) In addition, do more things that bring you pleasure and make you laugh and fewer activities that feel like obligations. Spend more time with people who make you feel good and less with people who are draining. Dwell more on what you like about yourself and less on what you see as your limitations. In short, have more fun! Make pleasure a priority instead of a luxury.

Allow yourself to accept nurturing and affection. If you didn't learn how to do this as a child, you may need to practice it. Every morning before you get up, spend a minute or two reveling in a memory of a time you felt loved. Do the same at night. Imagine your heart being filled with this love. Use affirmations that help you feel deserving of this nurturing and love.

Follow a healthy, whole foods diet with minimal sugar and adequate protein. (Every meal or snack should contain some protein.) Avoid caffeine because it whips your adrenals into a frenzy. Also avoid fasting or cleansing regimens because they can weaken you further.

Take a comprehensive multivitamin/mineral supplement.

Try herbal support, including:

- Licorice root: This herb contains plant hormones that mimic the effects of cortisol. Start with a small amount and gradually work up to one-quarter teaspoon solid licorice root extract three times per day.2 Make sure to monitor blood pressure, as licorice may increase blood pressure in susceptible individuals.

- Siberian ginseng: One of the components of Siberian ginseng is related to a precursor for DHEA and cortisol. Try one 100 mg capsule two times a day. It can have a stimulating effect, though, so if it interferes with your sleep, take it before three p.m.

Get plenty of sleep: Sleep is the most effective approach to high adrenaline levels. Many women require eight to ten hours of sleep to function optimally. Try to go to bed by ten P.M. Getting to sleep on the earlier side of midnight is much more restorative to your adrenals than sleep that begins later in the night, even if you sleep late the next morning to get in your full amount of sleep.

Exercise regularly. Regular light-to-moderate exercise is helpful, but not so much that you feel depleted afterward. Pushing yourself beyond your limits weakens your adrenals even further, so start slowly—even if it's only walking down your street and back. Then build up slowly.

Get more exposure to natural sunlight. This is not only good for your adrenal glands, but it boosts vitamin D, as well. Sunbathe only in the early morning or later afternoon, however, never in midday; and never get enough exposure to burn or even redden your skin. Work up to ten to fifteen minutes of exposure three to four times per week.

Prioritize. Make a list of your most important activities and commitments, and then let everything else go. Don't agree to a new task or commitment unless it's something that will recharge your batteries.

---

30 traits of an Empath

1. Knowing: Empaths just know stuff, without being told. It's a knowing that goes way beyond intuition or gut feelings, even though that ...is how many would describe the knowing. The more attuned they are the stronger this gift becomes.

2. Being in public places can be overwhelming: Places like shopping malls, supermarkets or stadiums where there are lots of people around can fill the empath with turbulently vexed emotions that are coming from others.

3. Feeling others emotions and taking them on as your own: This is a huge one for empaths. To some they will feel emotions off those near by and with others they will feel emotions from those a vast distance away, or both. The more adept empath will know if someone is having bad thoughts about them, even from great distance.

4. Watching violence, cruelty or tragedy on the TV is unbearable: The more attuned an empath becomes the worse it is and may make it so they eventually have to stop watching TV and reading newspapers altogether.

5. You know when someone is not being honest: If a friend or a loved one is telling you lies you know it (although many empaths try not to focus on this because knowing a loved one is lying can be painful). Or if someone is saying one thing but feeling/thinking another, you know.

6. Picking up physical symptoms off another: An empath will almost always develop the ailments off another (colds, eye infections, body aches and pains) especially those they're closest to, somewhat like sympathy pains.

7. Digestive disorders and lower back problems: The solar plexus chakra is based in the centre of the abdomen and it's known as the seat of emotions. This is where empaths feel the incoming emotion of another, which can weaken the area and eventually lead to anything from stomach ulcers to IBS (too many other conditions to list here). Lower back problems can develop from being ungrounded (amongst other things) and one, who has no knowledge of them being an empath, will almost always be ungrounded.

8. Always looking out for the underdog: Anyone whose suffering, in emotional pain or being bullied draws an empath's attention and compassion.

9. Others will want to offload their problems on you, even strangers: An empath can become a dumping ground for everyone else's issues and problems, which, if they're not careful can end up as their own.

10. Constant fatigue: Empaths often get drained of energy, either from energy vampires or just taking on too much from others, which even sleep will not cure. Many get diagnosed with ME.

11. Addictive personality: Alcohol, drugs, sex, are to name but a few addictions that empaths turn to, to block out the emotions of others. It is a form of self protection in order to hide from someone or something.

12. Drawn to healing, holistic therapies and all things metaphysical: Although many empaths would love to heal others they can end up turning away from being healers (even though they have a natural ability for it), after they've studied and qualified, because they take on too much from the one they are trying to heal. Especially if they are unaware of their empathy. Anything of a supernatural nature is of interest to empaths and they don't surprise or get shocked easily. Even at the revelation of what many others would consider unthinkable, for example, empaths would have known the world was round when others believed it was flat.

13. Creative: From singing, dancing, acting, drawing or writing an empath will have a strong creative streak and a vivid imagination.

14. Love of nature and animals: Being outdoors in nature is a must for empaths and pets are an essential part of their life.

15. Need for solitude: An empath will go stir-crazy if they don't get quiet time. This is even obvious in empathic children.

16. Gets bored or distracted easily if not stimulated: Work, school and home life has to be kept interesting for an empath or they switch off from it and end up daydreaming or doodling.

17. Finds it impossible to do things they don't enjoy: As above. Feels like they are living a lie by doing so. To force an empath to do something they dislike through guilt or labelling them as idle will only serve in making them unhappy. It's for this reason many empaths get labelled as being lazy.

18. Strives for the truth: This becomes more prevalent when an empath discovers his/her gifts and birthright. Anything untruthful feels plain wrong.

19. Always looking for the answers and knowledge: To have unanswered questions can be frustrating for an empath and they will endeavour to find an explanation. If they have a knowing about something they will look for confirmation. The downside to this is an information overload.

20. Likes adventure, freedom and travel: Empaths are free spirits.

21. Abhors clutter: It makes an empath feel weighed down and blocks the flow of energy.

22. Loves to daydream: An empath can stare into space for hours, in a world of their own and blissfully happy.

23. Finds routine, rules or control, imprisoning: Anything that takes away their freedom is debilitating to an empath even poisoning.

24. Prone to carry weight without necessarily overeating: The excess weight is a form of protection to stop the negative incoming energies having as much impact.

25. Excellent listener: An empath won't talk about themselves much unless it's to someone they really trust. They love to learn and know about others and genuinely care.

26. Intolerance to narcissism: Although kind and often very tolerant of others, empaths do not like to be around overly egotistical people, who put themselves first and refuse to consider another's feelings or points of view other than their own.

27. The ability to feel the days of the week: An empath will get the 'Friday Feeling' if they work Fridays or not. They pick up on how the collective are feeling. The first couple of days of a long, bank holiday weekend (Easter for example) can feel, to them, like the world is smiling, calm and relaxed. Sunday evenings, Mondays and Tuesdays, of a working week, have a very heavy feeling.

28. Will not choose to buy antiques, vintage or second-hand: Anything that's been pre-owned carries the energy of the previous owner. An empath will even prefer to have a brand new car or house (if they are in the financial situation to do so) with no residual energy.

29. Sense the energy of food: Many empaths don't like to eat meat or poultry because they can feel the vibrations of the animal (especially if the animal suffered), even if they like the taste.

30. Can appear moody, shy, aloof, disconnected: Depending on how an empath is feeling will depend on what face they show to the world. They can be prone to mood swings and if they've taken on too much negative will appear quiet and unsociable, even miserable. An empath detests having to pretend to be happy when they're sad, this only adds to their load (makes working in the service industry, when it's service with a smile, very challenging) and can make them feel like scuttling under a stone.

If you can say yes to most or all of the above then you are most definitely an empath

Empaths are having a particularly difficult time at the present time, picking up on all the negative emotions that are being emantated into the world from the populace.

TRAITS OF AN EMPATH by Christel Broederlow
Empaths are often quiet achievers. They can take a while to handle a compliment for they're more inclined to point out another's positive attributes. They are highly expressive in all areas of emotional connection, and talk openly, and, at times quite frankly. They may have few problems talking about their feelings if another cares to listen (regardless of how much they listen to others).

However, they can be the exact opposite: reclusive and apparently unresponsive at the best of times. They may even appear ignorant. Some are very good at "blocking out" others and that's not always a bad thing, at least for the learning empath struggling with a barrage of emotions from others, as well as their own feelings.

Empaths have a tendency to openly feel what is outside of them more so than what is inside of them. This can cause empaths to ignore their own needs. In general an empath is non-violent, non-aggressive and leans more towards being the peacemaker. Any area filled with disharmony creates an uncomfortable feeling in an empath. If they find themselves in the middle of a confrontation, they will endeavor to settle the situation as quickly as possible, if not avoid it all together. If any harsh words are expressed in defending themselves, they will likely resent their lack of self-control, and have a preference to peacefully resolve the problem quickly.

Empaths are more inclined to pick up another's feelings and project it back without realizing its origin in the first place. Talking things out is a major factor in releasing emotions in the learning empath. Empaths can develop an even stronger degree of understanding so that they can find peace in most situations. The downside is that empaths may bottle up emotions and build barriers sky-high so as to not let others know of their innermost thoughts and/or feelings. This withholding of emotional expression can be a direct result of a traumatic experience, an expressionless upbringing, or simply being told as a child, "Children are meant to be seen and not heard!"

Without a doubt, this emotional withholding can be detrimental to one's health, for the longer one's thoughts and/or emotions aren't released, the more power they build. The thoughts and/or emotions can eventually becoming explosive, if not crippling. The need to express oneself honestly is a form of healing and a choice open to all. To not do so can result in a breakdown of the person and result in mental/emotional instability or the creation of a physical ailment, illness or disease.

Empaths are sensitive to TV, videos, movies, news and broadcasts. Violence or emotional dramas depicting shocking scenes of physical or emotional pain inflicted on adults, children or animals can bring an empath easily to tears. At times, they may feel physically ill or choke back the tears. Some empaths will struggle to comprehend any such cruelty, and may have grave difficulty in expressing themselves in the face of another's ignorance, closed-mindedness and obvious lack of compassion. They simply cannot justify the suffering they feel and see.

You will find empaths working with people, animals or nature with a true passion and dedication to help them. They are often tireless teachers and/or caretakers for our environment and all within it. Many volunteers are empathic and give up personal time to help others without pay and/or recognition.

Empaths may be excellent storytellers due to an endless imagination, inquisitive minds and ever-expanding knowledge. They can be old romantics at heart and very gentle. They may also be the "keepers" of ancestral knowledge and family history. If not the obvious family historians, they may be the ones who listen to the stories passed down and possess the majority of the family history. Not surprisingly, they may have started or possess a family tree.

They have a broad interest in music to suit their many expressive temperaments, and others can query how empaths can listen to one style of music, and within minutes, change to something entirely different. Lyrics within a song can have adverse, powerful effects on empaths, especially if it is relevant to a recent experience. In these moments, it is advisable for empaths to listen to music without lyrics, to avoid playing havoc with their emotions!

They are just as expressive with body language as with words, thoughts, and feelings. Their creativity is often expressed through dance, acting, and bodily movements. Empaths can project an incredible amount of energy portraying and/or releasing emotion. Empaths can become lost in the music, to the point of being in a trance-like state; they become one with the music through the expression of their physical bodies. They describe this feeling as a time when all else around them is almost non-existent.

People of all walks of life and animals are attracted to the warmth and genuine compassion of empaths. Regardless of whether others are aware of one being empathic, people are drawn to them as a metal object is to a magnet!

Even complete strangers find it easy to talk to empaths about the most personal things, and before they know it, they have poured out their hearts and souls without intending to do so consciously. It is as though on a sub-conscious level that person knows instinctively that empaths would listen with compassionate understanding. Then again, for empaths, it is always nice to actually be heard themselves!

Here are the listeners of life. They can be outgoing, bubbly, enthusiastic and a joy to be in the presence of, as well as highly humorous at the most unusual moments! On the flip side, empaths can be weighted with mood swings that will have others around them want to jump overboard and abandon ship! The thoughts and feelings empaths receive from any and all in their life can be so overwhelming (if not understood) that their moods can fluctuate with lightning speed. One moment they may be delightfully happy and with a flick of the switch, miserable.

Abandoning an empath in the throes of alternating moods can create detrimental effects. A simple return of empathic love–listening and caring compassionately without bias, judgment and/or condemnation–can go an incredibly long way to an empath's instant recovery. Many empaths don't understand what is occurring within them. They literally have no idea that another person's emotions are now felt, as one's own and reflected outwardly. They are confused as to how one moment all was well, and then the next, they feel so depressed, alone, etc. The need to understand the possibilities of empath connection is a vital part of the empaths journey for themselves and for those around them.

Empaths are often problem solvers, thinkers, and studiers of many things. As far as empaths are concerned, where a problem is, so too is the answer. They often will search until they find one – if only for peace of mind. This can certainly prove beneficial for others in their relationships, in the workplace, or on the home front. Where there is a will, there is a way and the empath will find it. The empath can literally (likely without the knowledge of what's actually occurring) tap into Universal Knowledge and be receptive to guidance in solving anything they put their head and hearts into.

Empaths often are vivid and/or lucid dreamers. They can dream in detail and are inquisitive of dream content. Often they feel as though the dreams are linked to their physical life somehow, and not just a mumble of nonsensical, irrelevant, meaningless images. This curiosity will lead many empathic dreamers to unravel some of the "mysterious" dream contents from an early age and connect the interpretation to its relevance in their physical life. If not, they may be led to dream interpretations through other means.

Empaths are daydreamers with difficulty keeping focused on the mundane. If life isn't stimulating, off an empath will go into a detached state of mind. They will go somewhere, anywhere, in a thought that appears detached from the physical reality, yet is alive and active for they really are off and away. If a tutor is lecturing with little to no emotional input, empaths will not be receptive to such teaching and can (unintentionally) drift into a state of daydreaming.

Give the empath student the tutor who speaks with stimuli and emotion (through actual experience of any given subject) and the empath is receptively alert. Empaths are a captivated audience. This same principle applies in acting. An actor will either captivate the audience through expressing (in all aspects) emotions (as though they really did experience the role they are portraying) or will loose them entirely. Empaths make outstanding actors.

Empaths frequently experience déjà vu and synchronicities. What may initially start as, "Oh, what a coincidence", will lead to the understanding of synchronicities as an aspect of who they are. These synchronicities will become a welcomed and continually expanding occurrence. As an understanding of self grows, the synchronicities become more fluent and free flowing. The synchronicities can promote a feeling of euphoria as empaths identify with them and appreciate the connection to their empathic nature.

Empaths are most likely to have had varying paranormal experiences throughout their lives. NDE's (Near death experiences) and or OBE's (Out of body experiences) can catapult an unaware empath into the awakening period and provide the momentum for a journey of discovery. Those who get caught up in life, in society's often dictating ways, in work etc., can become lost in a mechanical way of living that provides very little meaning. All "signs of guidance" are ignored to shift out of this state of "doing". A path to being whole again becomes evident and a search for more meaning in one's life begins.

These types of experiences appear dramatic, can be life-altering indeed, and are most assuredly just as intensely memorable in years to come. They are the voice of guidance encouraging us to pursue our journey in awareness. Sometimes, some of us require that extra assistance!

For some empaths, the lack of outside understanding towards paranormal events they experience, may lead to suppressing such abilities. (Most of these abilities are very natural and not a coincidence.) Empaths may unknowingly adopt the positive or negative attitude of others as their own. (This, however, can be overcome.) Empaths may need to follow interests in the paranormal and the unexplained with curiosity so as to explain and accept their life circumstances.

The Mind Unleashed
www.TheMindUnleashed.org

Honey and Cinnamon:

It is found that a mix of honey and cinnamon cures most diseases. Honey is produced in most of the countries of the world. Scientists of today also note honey as very effective medicine for all kinds of diseases. Honey can be used without side effects which is also a plus. Today's science says that even though honey is sweet, when it is taken in the right dosage as a medicine, it does not harm even diabetic patients. Researched by western scientists:

HEART DISEASES: Make a paste of honey and cinnamon powder, put it on toast instead of jelly and jam and eat it regularly for breakfast. It reduces the cholesterol and could potentially save one from heart attack. Also, even if you have already had an attack studies show you could be kept miles away from the next attack. Regular use of cinnamon honey strengthens the heart beat. In America and Canada, various nursing homes have treated patients successfully and have found that as one ages the arteries and veins lose their flexibility and get clogged; honey and cinnamon revitalize the arteries and the veins.

ARTHRITIS: Arthritis patients can benefit by taking one cup of hot water with two tablespoons of honey and one small teaspoon of cinnamon powder. When taken daily even chronic arthritis can be cured. In a recent research conducted at the Copenhagen University, it was found that when the doctors treated their patients with a mixture of one tablespoon Honey and half teaspoon Cinnamon powder before breakfast, they found that within a week (out of the 200 people so treated) practically 73 patients were totally relieved of pain -- and within a month, most all the patients who could not walk or move around because of arthritis now started walking without pain.

BLADDER INFECTIONS: Take two tablespoons of cinnamon powder and one teaspoon of honey in a glass of lukewarm water and drink it. It destroys the germs in the bladder....who knew?

CHOLESTEROL: Two tablespoons of honey and three teaspoons of Cinnamon Powder mixed in 16 ounces of tea water given to a cholesterol patient was found to reduce the level of cholesterol in the blood by 10 percent within two hours. As mentioned for arthritic patients, when taken three times a day, any chronic cholesterol-could be cured. According to information received in the said Journal, pure honey taken with food daily relieves complaints of cholesterol.

COLDS: Those suffering from common or severe colds should take one tablespoon lukewarm honey with 1/4 spoon cinnamon powder daily for three days. This process will cure most chronic cough, cold, and, clear the sinuses, and it's delicious too!

UPSET STOMACH: Honey taken with cinnamon powder cures stomach ache and also is said to clear stomach ulcers from its root.

GAS: According to the studies done in India and Japan, it is revealed that when Honey is taken with cinnamon powder the stomach is relieved of gas.

IMMUNE SYSTEM: Daily use of honey and cinnamon powder strengthens the immune system and protects the body from bacterial and viral attacks. Scientists have found that honey has various vitamins and iron in large amounts. Constant use of Honey strengthens the white blood corpuscles (where DNA is contained) to fight bacterial and viral diseases.

INDIGESTION: Cinnamon powder sprinkled on two tablespoons of honey taken before food is eaten relieves acidity and digests the heaviest of meals

INFLUENZA: A scientist in Spain has proved that honey contains a natural 'Ingredient' which kills the influenza germs and saves the patient from flu.

LONGEVITY: Tea made with honey and cinnamon powder, when taken regularly, arrests the ravages of old age. Use four teaspoons of honey, one teaspoon of cinnamon powder, and three cups of boiling water to make a tea. Drink 1/4 cup, three to four times a day. It keeps the skin fresh and soft and arrests old age. Life spans increase and even a 100 year old will start performing the chores of a 20-year-old.

RASPY OR SORE THROAT: When throat has a tickle or is raspy, take one tablespoon of honey and sip until gone. Repeat every three hours until throat is without symptoms.

PIMPLES: Three tablespoons of honey and one teaspoon of cinnamon powder paste. Apply this paste on the pimples before sleeping and wash it off the next morning with warm water. When done daily for two weeks, it removes all pimples from the root.

SKIN INFECTIONS:Applying honey and cinnamon powder in equal parts on the affected parts cures eczema, ringworm and all types of skin Infections.

WEIGHT LOSS: Daily in the morning one half hour before breakfast and on an empty stomach, and at night before sleeping, drink 1 tsp honey and 1/2 tsp cinnamon powder added to one cup of hot/warm water. When taken regularly, it reduces the weight of even the most obese person. Also, drinking this mixture regularly does not allow the fat to accumulate in the body even though the person may eat a high calorie diet.

CANCER: Recent research in Japan and Australia has revealed that advanced cancer of the stomach and bones have been cured successfully. Patients suffering from these kinds of cancer should daily take one tablespoon of honey with one teaspoon of cinnamon powder three times a day for one month.

FATIGUE: Recent studies have shown that the sugar content of honey is more helpful rather than being detrimental to the strength of the body. Senior citizens who take honey and cinnamon powder in equal parts are more alert and flexible. Dr. Milton, who has done research, says that a half tablespoon of honey taken in a glass of water and sprinkled with cinnamon powder, even when the vitality of the body starts to decrease, when taken daily after brushing and in the afternoon at about 3:00 P.M., the vitality of the body increases within a week.

BAD BREATH: People of South America, gargle with one teaspoon of honey and cinnamon powder mixed in hot water first thing in the morning so their breath stays fresh throughout the day.

HEARING LOSS: Daily morning and night honey and cinnamon powder, taken in equal parts restores hearing.
THE HONEY NEEDS TO BE A LOCAL RAW HONEY NOT STORE BOUGHT. CINNAMON NEEDS TO BE PURE CINNAMON

UNE 6, 2014 by KAREN FOSTER
How To Eliminate Candida Naturally

An imbalance in gut flora can allow specific bacteria and fungi to invade our bodies. Candida is a fungus, which is a form of yeast, and a very small amount of it lives in your mouth and intestines. When overgrowth overgrowth occurs, candida breaks down the wall of the intestine and penetrates the bloodstream, releasing toxic byproducts into your body. This can lead to many different health problems, ranging from digestive issues to depression and even cancer.

How do you get candida overgrowth?

The healthy bacteria in your gut typically keep your candida levels in check. However, several factors can cause the candida population to get out of hand:
Eating a diet high in refined carbohydrates and sugar (which feed the yeast)
Consuming a lot of alcohol
Taking oral contraceptives
Living a high-stress lifestyle
Taking a round of antibiotics that killed too many of those friendly bacteria

Symptoms Caused by Candida Overgrowth
When Candida Albicans is under control it poses no problem, but when it gets out of control it begins to overgrow causing numerous symptoms and health problems from the top of the head to the tips of the toes, from migraines to nail fungus. It can result in symptoms inside (pain and malfunction of organs, even brain lesions) and outside (eczema and hives). It can also cause problems with the mind and emotions. Here are many of the symptoms caused by an overproduction of candida.
Allergies, sensitivities and intolerances that worsen in damp, muggy or moldy places or weather that is damp, muggy, humid or rainy.
Hay fever and asthma.
Intolerances or allergies to perfumes, odors, fumes, fabric shop odors, grass, cats, dogs or other animals, tobacco smoke, chemicals, smog, molds, dust mites, dust, pollen, and other airborne substances.
Athletes' foot.
Babies - colic, diaper rash, thrush (coated white tongue), and cradle cap.
Bruising easily.
Cheekbone or forehead tenderness, pain.
Cold hands or feet, low body temperature.
Cold-like symptoms - excessive mucus in the sinuses, nose, throat, bronchial tubes and lungs.
Cravings or addictions for sugar, bread, pasta and other high carb foods, and also alcohol.

Cysts, abnormal formation of, in different parts of the body, especially around the neck, throat, and ovaries, and in the bladder or scrotum.

Digestive problems - diarrhea, constipation, abdominal distention, bloating or pain, gas, mucus in the stools, hiatal hernia, ulcers, suffering from bacteria, i.e. salmonella, E. coli, h. pylori, etc.

Ears - ringing in the ears (tinnitus), sounds in the ears, ear infections, dryness, itchiness, ear pain, ear aches, ear discharges, fluid in ears, deafness, abnormal wax build-up.

Eyes - erratic vision, spots in front of eyes (eye floaters) and flashing lights; redness, dryness, itching, excessive tearing, inability to tear, etc.

Fatigue, chronic fatigue syndrome or Epstein Barr or a feeling of being drained of energy, lethargy, drowsiness.

Flu-like symptoms.

Glands swollen, too little saliva (dryness in the mouth), blocked salivary glands, swollen lymph nodes.

Hair loss, scum on the scalp, dandruff, itchy scalp, scalp sores and dryness.

Heart palpitations and irregular heart beat.

Headaches, migraines, brain fog, dizziness, etc.

Hemorrhoids, and rectal itching, rash, irritation and redness.

Hypoglycemia (low blood sugar), and diabetes.

Hypothyroidism, Wilson's Thyroid Syndrome, Hashimoto's disease, hyperthyroidism, erratic thyroid function, etc.

Irritability, nervousness, jitteriness and panic attacks.

Lesions on the skin, and inside the body, i.e. the brain.

Male associated problems - jock itch, loss of sex drive, impotence, prostitis, penis infections, difficulty urinating, urinary frequency or urgency, painful intercourse, swollen scrotum, etc.

Female health problems - infertility, vaginitis, unusual odors, endometriosis (irregular or painful menstruation), cramps, menstrual irregularities, pre-menstrual syndrome (PMS), discharge, painful intercourse, loss of sexual drive, redness or swelling of the vulva and surrounding area, vaginal itching or thrush, burning or redness, or persistent infections.

Fungal infections of the skin or nails, i.e. ringworm, saborrheic dermatitis, dark and light patches on the skin (tinea versicolor), etc.

Joint pain, stiffness or swelling (arthritis).

Kidney and bladder - infections, cystitis (inflammation of the bladder with possible infection), urinary frequency or urgency, low urine output, smelly urine, difficulty urinating, burning pain when urinating.

Lack of appetite.

Mind and Mood - anxiety attacks, crying spells, memory loss, feeling spaced out, depression(including suicidal feelings), manic feelings, inability to concentrate, mood swings, irritability, etc.

Mouth sores or blisters, canker sores, dryness, bad breath, a white coating on the tongue (thrush) and blocked salivary glands.

Muscle aches and pain, numbness, burning or tingling, and lack of strength and coordination.

Nasal congestion, postnasal drip, itching, dryness.

Odor of the feet, hair or body not relieved by washing.

Respiratory - cough, bronchitis or pneumonia, pain or tightness in the chest, wheezing, shortness of breath, asthma.

Sick all over feeling.

Sinus inflammation, swelling and infections.

Skin - dryness, dry red patches, acne, pimples, hives, rashes, itching skin, eczema, psoriasis, seborrhoea, ringworm, contact dermatitis, rosacea, etc.

Stomach - h.pylori bacteria (causes ulcers), heartburn, indigestion, hiatal hernia, acid reflux, belching, vomiting, burning, stomach pains, needle-like pains, food that seems to sit in the stomach like a lump, etc.

Sleep - insomnia, waking up frequently, nightmares, restless sleep, etc.

Sore throat, hoarse voice, constant tickle in the throat, laryngitis (loss of voice), etc.

What Causes Candida to Get Out of Control?

The causes of immune system dysfunction are varied and complex, but antibiotics are the biggest culprits because they wipe out friendly micro-organisms, in the digestive system. Because Candida is resistant to antibiotics the imbalance of micro-organisms allows it to take over. It begins to change its shape and starts to overgrow; raising large families called colonies.

Adding to the problem of malabsorption are nutritional deficiencies that also weaken the immune system. Today's standard diet lacks the necessary nutrients to maintain a healthy immune system. It is loaded with sugar, carbohydrates, hydrogenated oils and fats (trans-fats), white flour products, processed foods, food additives, preservatives, pesticides, and heavy metals. This, in addition to foods being irradiated (exposed to high levels of radiation to extend shelf life), and being grown in nutrient depleted soil, long storage and transportation time, and improper handling, cooking and microwaving that goes on in most homes, further depletes nutrients available. All of these factors contribute to a weakened immune system.

Testing for Candida at Home

Your holistic practitioner will have conclusive means of testing for candida, however for a simple at home test try the following. First thing in the morning, before you put anything in your mouth, fill a clear glass with room temperature bottled water.

Work up a bit of saliva, and spit it into the glass of water. Check the water every 15 minutes or so for up to one hour.

If you see strings (fibers) traveling down into the water from the saliva floating on the top, cloudy specks (particles suspended in the water) or cloudy saliva that sinks to the bottom of the glass you have a candida problem.

The Candida Control Program

In order to get Candida overgrowth under control five things need to be done simultaneously:

1. Eliminate foods that feed Candida

Candida overgrowth is mainly fueled by sugar, refined carbohydrates and gluten. Let's look at each of these separately so you know what to avoid exactly.

Candida's main food supply is sugar and all forms of it, such as lactose contained in dairy products, honey, glucose, fructose, and sugar substitutes, i.e. Nutrasweet, aspartame, saccharin. Eliminating sugar is the most important part of the Candida Program. All fruit, except lemons, are also very high in sugar and should be extremely limited during the initial stages of the program, along with some vegetables that are very high in sugar, such as sweet potatoes, parsnips and beets.

Sugar also contained is most processed foods such as smoked luncheon meats, ketchup, cereal, and yogurt making it important to read labels carefully.

Most Candida sufferers are gluten intolerant. Gluten is an elastic and gluey protein found in wheat, rye, barley, oats, spelt, kamut, triticale and it is hidden in an endless variety of processed foods. Triticale is a new hybrid grain with the properties of wheat and rye, while spelt and kamut are gluten-containing wheat variants and are likely to cause problems similar to other wheat varieties. Gluten-containing grains have come to be used extensively in breads and other baked goods because of their "glutinous," sticky consistency.

Gluten grains feed Candida because they have a high glycemic index just like sugar, and like sugar, creates insulin resistance within the cells which leads to blood sugar problems like hypoglycemia and diabetes. The cells become resistant to insulin as they try to protect themselves from the toxic effective of high doses of insulin caused by high intake of sugar and simple carbohydrates. As the cells become insulin resistant, the pancreas produces more insulin which creates a vicious cycle. This exhausts the pancreas eventually leading to its breakdown resulting in diabetes.

Gluten grains contain a protein that is difficult to digest and interferes with mineral absorption and causes intestinal damage. This damage makes the intestines incapable of absorbing nutrients such as proteins, carbohydrates, fats, vitamins, minerals, and even water in some cases. Our grain food supply also contains mycotoxins (a toxin produced by a fungus), especially found in corn and wheat. Mycotoxins can suppress our normal immune function. See the section on Yeast, Mold and Fungus for more information.

2. Build up the immune system

Eating the right foods
Taking essential supplements
Avoiding yeast, mold and fungus

If the wrong diet is constantly consumed, or if yeast overgrowth damage is never reversed from previous drug and antibiotic use, a cure can almost never be achieved. Eating the right foods is the most important aspect of getting Candida under control and building up the immune system. The "Candida Control Diet" is high in protein and good saturated fats and oils, and low in carbohydrates, and contains no sugars, grains or processed foods. All foods must be as fresh and natural as possible, and free of additives, pesticides, heavy metals, irradiation, mycotoxins, etc.

Good Fats and Oils - Good fats and oils are equally important to protein in the diet and they are essential to getting Candida under control. They not only increase the body's ability to absorb nutrients from the foods eaten but also provide the most efficient source of energy. They also provide the building blocks for cell membranes and a variety of hormones and hormone-like substances. Good fats act as carriers for important fat-soluble vitamins A, D, E and K and for the conversion of carotene to vitamin A, for mineral absorption and for a host of other processes. The kinds of fats consumed greatly influence the assimilation and utilization of vitamin D.

Essential Fatty Acids - There are also two types of essential fatty acids that must be obtained from the diet and these are omega-3s and omega-6s. They are called essential because we have to get them from food because our bodies can't manufacture them from other fats. Most people's diets contain an excessive amount of omega 6 fats, therefore it is important to ensure the diet contains more omega 3 rich foods to offset this imbalance.

Avoid all newfangled fats and oils (trans fats) - Candida sufferers cannot afford to jeopardize their health by consuming toxic oils and fats and must avoid all of the newfangled polyunsaturated fats and hydrogenated vegetable oils (margarine, Canola oil, safflower oil, etc.), called trans fats. These newfangled fats and oils are not only toxic and increase the body's need for vitamin E and other antioxidants, but also depress the immune system. All trans fats, found in margarine and shortenings used in most commercial baked goods and most processed food, should always be avoided even by healthy people.
Coconut Oil - Coconut oil is another healthy saturated fat that contains many properties that are beneficial to Candida sufferers which are anti-bacterial, anti-viral and anti-fungal. It also kills off yeast overgrowth. Coconut oil supports immune system function, supplies important nutrients necessary for good health and improves digestion and nutrient absorption.

The fat in coconut oil is easily digested and absorbed, unlike the newfangled trans fats that act like plastic in the body. It puts little strain on the digestive system and provides a quick source of energy necessary to promote healing. Coconut oil is absorbed directly from the intestines into the portal vein and sent straight to the liver, whereas other fats require pancreatic enzymes to break them into smaller units.

Avoid Soybean and Soy-based foods - Soybeans contains large quantities of natural toxins or "anti-nutrients," including potent enzyme inhibitors that block the action of enzymes needed for protein digestion. These inhibitors are not completely deactivated during ordinary cooking and can produce serious gastric distress, reduced protein digestion and chronic deficiencies in amino acid (proteins) uptake. In test animals, diets high in enzyme inhibitors cause enlargement and pathological conditions of the pancreas, thyroid malfunction and other diseases including cancer. Soybeans also contain haemagglutinin, a clot-promoting substance that causes red blood cells to clump together.

Soy also contains one of the highest percentages of pesticides of any of our foods and is 99% genetically modified. Soybeans are also high in phytic acid, present in the bran or hulls of all seeds, which blocks the uptake of essential minerals - calcium, magnesium, copper, iron and especially zinc - in the intestinal tract. Candida sufferers must avoid soy and all soy products in order to get well.

Taking essential supplements

Candida sufferers need to build up their immune system by supplementing with certain essential vitamins and minerals, that are yeast-free and sugar-free, including:

Chlorella is a whole-food that contains a wide array of vitamins, minerals and enzymes. It helps build the immune system, detoxifies heavy metals and other pesticides in the body, improves the digestive system, improves energy levels and normalize blood sugar and blood pressure. Take two capsules three times a day.
Vitamin B Complex (non-yeast), 50 mgs. twice a day.
Vitamin C with bioflavonoids, 1,000 mgs. twice a day.

Vitamin D (with vitamin A) - take 1 teaspoon per 50 lbs. of body weight per day of a high quality cod liver oil or fish oil.

Vitamin E, containing natural alpha tocopherol, (d-alpha tocopherol is synthetic), that is not from a soy source, 400 IU twice a day.

Calcium/Magnesium Citrate, with "elemental amounts" containing 800-1,200 mgs. of calcium with an equal ratio of magnesium.

3. Kill off Candida overgrowth

There are many anti-fungal agents that kill off Candida overgrowth, including raw garlic, apple cider vinegar, olive leaf extract and Pau d'arco.

Garlic - Garlic contains a large number of sulphur containing compounds that exhibit very potent broad-spectrum anti-fungal properties. Among the most studied are allicin, alliin, alliinase and S-allylcysteine.

Fresh garlic is significantly more potent against Candida albicans than any other form, including tablets, oils and pills. Fresh garlic is also a suitable alternative to drugs for serious systemic yeast infections in patients with severe immune suppression. Adding fresh garlic to food (raw and crushed), or crushing and swallowing raw clove is a cheap and powerful anti-fungal treatment. Garlic also stimulates the immune system, improves circulation, lowers high blood pressure, kills intestinal parasites, and is a powerful antioxidant and antibiotic, in addition to many other health benefits.

To obtain the most benefit from garlic buy certified organic garlic and crush it. Crushing breaks the cell walls releasing garlic's beneficial properties. To kill off Candida overgrowth take 4-5 average sized cloves per day mixed in foods or with meals. Another alternative is to drink 3-4 cups of garlic tea per day.

Raw apple cider vinegar - Raw apple cider vinegar and Candida do not get along. Take a tablespoon of apple cider vinegar and mix it with a glass of water and drink before every meal. The apple cider vinegar helps to fight off the intestinal yeast overgrowth by actually killing the yeast, creating a die off reaction. Raw unfiltered apple cider vinegar creates an unfriendly environment for the yeast, while helping create a good environment for friendly gut flora.

Olive Leaf Extract - Olive leaf extract can kill invading fungus rather than just inhibiting its growth. It contains a a phenolic compound called oleuropein, which has antiviral, anti-fungal, antiprotozoal, and antibacterial properties. Take as directed on the product label.

Pau d'arco - Pau d'arco is the bark of a rainforest tree which is inherently anti-fungal (also known as Taheebo or Lepacho tea). Pau d'arco may be taken in a capsule or a tea. Take capsules as directed on the product label or drink 3 cups of tea per day.

4. Plant good bacteria in the digestive tract

As the yeast overgrowth is being killed off by anti-fungal agents it is important to ingest a constant supply of probiotics. These are the 'friendly' or 'beneficial' bacteria, or micro organisms, that live in the digestive tract. As yeast colonies are reduced space becomes available for colonizing the other healthy bacteria. The most numerous bacteria found in the small intestines are species of Lactobacilli. In the colon the majority are mainly Bifidobacteria.

The easiest and least expensive way to plant healthy bacteria in the digestive tract is to take Cabbage Rejuvelac. But probiotic supplements can also plant good bacteria in the digestive tract. Unfortunately it's not as simple as just buying the first probiotic supplement and assuming it will do the job. The best probiotic supplements will contain specific strains of bacteria that have been studied and verified as effective, and they will identified on the bottle as a series of letters or numbers after the name of the bacteria to indicate a specific strain. Some of the most studied strains include Lactobacillus acidophilus DDS-1 and Lactobacillus GG. Probiotic supplements should be at least 500 billion organisms per gram, contained in dark bottles to avoid deterioration by heat and light, and kept refrigerated, even in the store. Take according to instructions on the bottle.

5. Manage the healing crisis

The Healing Crisis is brought about when the body becomes overcrowded with waste and toxins. Cells and tissues begin to throw off the waste and carry it from the bloodstream to various eliminating organs including the bowels, kidneys, lungs, skin, nasal passages, ears, throat, and genital organs. These organs in turn become congested and irritated producing symptoms such as colds, boils, kidney and bladder infections, headaches, open sores, diarrhea and fevers.

Die-off symptoms are caused by high numbers of yeast being killed off which releases a high number toxins into the system. In medical terms this is called the Herxheimer's reaction, or yeast die-off phenomenon. Die-off symptoms resembles the flu and can be very uncomfortable. They can be alleviated by:

Taking 1,000 mgs of Vitamin C (preferably in powdered form in pure water) several times a day or whenever needed.
Taking an Epsom salts bath also draws toxins out through the skin and helps minimized die-off symptoms (add two cups, or 500 grams, of Epsom salts to warm bath water).

The most important aspect of the healing crisis is to never go to extremes in making changes to your diet or lifestyle. It is important to gradually introduce changes one at a time, allowing the body to adapt to the changes and adjust itself. The keys to successfully overcoming Candida are: 1) sticking to the Candida Control Program, 2) being patient, and 3) being persistent. You will get well.

Drink More Buttermilk

Undoubtedly considered as the best summer soother, buttermilk or chaanch is a wonder drink that goes beyond quenching your thirst and refreshing you. Being a by-product of the process of churning cream into butter, most of the beneficial properties associated with milk are retained in buttermilk too.

Great for your skin
Buttermilk contains large amounts of lactic acid, an Alpha Hydroxy Acid (AHA), which is part of several expensive beauty products and treatments.
Effective treatment for sunburn

Buttermilk acts as a natural lotion that helps soothe sunburn. Simply mix buttermilk with tomato juice, and apply this mixture on the affected area.

Anti-ageing benefits

Buttermilk mixed with honey works as a great anti-ageing solution.

Keeps weight under control

Buttermilk is lower in fat and calories compared to milk. Apart from that, it can make you feel full for a long period of time, making you feel less hungry.

Keeps body heat under check

This has been one of the favourite reasons to consume buttermilk for ages. Buttermilk helps cool down your body temperatures.

Best for your digestive system

Buttermilk is a natural probiotic, which means that it provides the "gut friendly" bacteria that aid in digestion. It also helps to reduce frequent heartburn, and regulates the acidity that usually follows a spicy meal.

Packed with nutrients

Buttermilk is low in calories, but high in several essential nutrients like vitamin B12, calcium, phosphorus and riboflavin. These nutrients work together to promote healthy bones, skin and immunity

---

Cannabis and Coconut Oil

Medical marijuana capsules infused in coconut oil are an alternative way to therapeutically use cannabis without having to inhale it through smoking. Infusing cannabis into coconut oil also allows for easy entry into the liver where it can be rapidly processed.

Coconut oil is used because of its high amount of essential fatty acids which makes it a good binding agent for the cannabinoids. Not to mention its amazing health properties. Half of the fat in coconut oil is comprised of a fat that is not frequently found in nature, lauric acid.

Lauric acid has been called a "miracle" ingredient due to its health promoting capabilities and is present in a mother's milk. In fact, it can be found in only three dietary sources—small amounts in butterfat and larger amounts in palm kernel and coconut oil.

In the body, lauric acid is converted to monolaurin, which is a potent antiviral, antibacterial and antiprotozoal substance. Because monolaurin is a monoglyceride, it can destroy lipid-coated viruses including measles, influenza, HIV, herpes and a number of pathogenic bacteria.

About the author:

Orisol Brillanti (Facebook name)

I see Light, I see Love, the Unconditional Love for all Humanity, not for the humans of now but for the eternal Humanity of past, present and future. There is always a deeper vision, a cosmic essence in your thoughts, in your writings. There is also an integral Unconditional Love for all Creation, for all realms. The wise doctor is always there, giving advice about preventing illness and curing the integral being (soul, mind, spirit, body). And all this Pradeep does selflessly, just serving a Greatest Purpose.

And, what to say about the philosopher? His ideas are being delivered from a profound multidimensional viewpoint but in a simple language. And all of the above always imbued with art and touched with a smart sense of humor. Sometimes I have felt sadness in him, yes, because Pradeep would like a more Humane and beautiful world. However, The Light is always, always there in his writings.

Thanks Pradeep for our friendship!

My other books (Pradeep Maheshwari):

Life is a Pilgrimage.

- This book is a diary of sorts, from a father to his daughter. All the memories of childhood in pictures along with the messages a father ought to be teaching his child so that later in life the child does not have to learn everything from scratch the hard way. A record of life that was; of which the children normally do not retain memories. In this book I am preserving the memories and passing all the pragmatic lessons I learnt from life.
- In USA, on Amazon USA it is sold as **The Pragmatic Yogi**
- In Amazon Europe is is available as Life is a Pilgrimage
  List Price: **$30.00**
  8" x 10" (20.32 x 25.4 cm) Full Color on White paper 132 pages
  ISBN-13: **978-1500843090** ISBN-10: **1500843091**
  BISAC: Psychology / Education & Training
- IN Amazon USA – **The Pragmatic Yogi:**
List Price: **$30.00**

8" x 10" (20.32 x 25.4 cm)   Full Color on White paper   134 pages

ISBN-13: 978-1500857202   ISBN-10: 1500857203
BISAC: Psychology / Applied Psychology

- *On Kindle : File size 64144 KB*

ASIN: B00MRLYHQ8

- It can be seen on **ISSUU** at:

http://issuu.com/pradeeppkmaheshwari/docs/scribd_-_life_is_a_pilgrimage-/0

- It is also on **Scribd** at:

http://www.scribd.com/doc/236797843/Life-is-a-Pilgrimage

1)a

Soul Repair thru Art Therapy: The Science of Self rediscovery through Art Therapy

Authored by Mr Pradeep Maheshwari

List Price: $14.00
8" x 10" (20.32 x 25.4 cm)
Black & White on White paper
274 pages
ISBN-13: 978-1500488000
ISBN-10: 1500488003
BISAC: Psychology / Applied Psychology
The Science of Self rediscovery through Art Therapy leading to a deeper understanding to the solutions to disturbed mind-states and their causes. Helping others realize their full potential through ART by making their art a reflection of their own persona and thereby assist them to discover equilibrium in life and the truth of their own being.
1b. Also available on kindle

Product Details

- **File Size:** 654 KB

- **Print Length:** 168 pages

- **Sold by:** Amazon Digital Services, Inc.

- **Language:** English

- **ASIN:** B00LQM082Q

1c – PDF file on Request Rs 200

1d – On Scribd –

http://www.scribd.com/doc/233560053/Soul-Repair-Thru-Art-Interior-for-Kindle

2) a
Yogic-Spiritual Principles in Applied Psychology: (the book SOUL REPAIR THRU ART THERAPY is included in this volume)
Achieving Perfect Parenting, Effective teaching & Meaningful Counseling

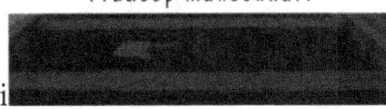

Authored by Mr Pradeep PK Maheshwari

List Price: $18.00
8" x 10" (20.32 x 25.4 cm)
Black & White on White paper
384 pages
ISBN-13: 978-1500660765
ISBN-10: 1500660760
BISAC: Psychology / Social Psychology

2b Also available on Kindle
Product Details

- **File Size:** 2965 KB

- **Print Length:** 258 pages

- **Sold by:** Amazon Digital Services, Inc.

- **Language:** English

- **ASIN:** B00M6KGG28

2c – PDF file available for Rs 300.

2d: **On Scribd**:
http://www.scribd.com/doc/235153871/Yogic-Spiritual-Principles-in-Applied-Psychology

3a
Kindness, Medicine and this Business of Life.
A small expose on what makes us tick and how it affects our health and well being.

Authored by Mr Pradeep Maheshwari

List Price: $12.00
8" x 10" (20.32 x 25.4 cm)
Black & White on White paper
206 pages
ISBN-13: 978-1500665074
ISBN-10: 150066507X
BISAC: Body, Mind & Spirit / Inspiration & Personal Growt

3b also on Kindle
Product Details

- **File Size:** 1664 KB

- **Print Length:** 174 pages

- **Sold by:** Amazon Digital Services, Inc.

- **Language:** English

- **ASIN:** B00M79K13I

3c PDF file available for Rs 200

3d: **On Scribd** –
http://www.scribd.com/doc/235253923/Kindness-Medicine-the-Business-of-Life